As Mormonism spreads throughout America, evangelical Christians need to be prepared to confront Mormons with the Gospel of Christ. In **Have You Witnessed to a Mormon Lately?**, James Spencer carefully examines the errors of Mormonism, presents tactics for defending Christian truths, and reveals specific strategies for witnessing to Mormons. With this practical guide, you'll find the information and encouragement you need to meet the challenge presented by the "Latter Day Saints."

About the Author:

James Spencer, an evangelical pastor, has written and lectured extensively on Mormonism and is a widely recognized authority in this area. Before he accepted Christ as his Savior, Jim Spencer was a missionary and Elder in the Mormon Church. His story is told in his first book, *Beyond Mormonism: An Elder's Story.* Jim lives in Idaho Falls, Idaho, with his wife, Margaretta, and two daughters.

Have you Witnessed to a Mormon Lately?

James R. Spencer

Published by
chosen books

FLEMING H. REVELL COMPANY
OLD TAPPAN, NEW JERSEY

Some of the names in this book have been changed to protect the privacy of the people involved.

Unless otherwise indicated, the Bible translation quoted is the *New International Version*, copyright © 1978 by New York International Bible Society. Italics have been added by the author.

Library of Congress Cataloging in Publication Data

Spencer, James R.   Have you witnessed to a Mormon lately?

   "A Chosen book"—T.p. verso.
   Includes bibliographical references.
   1. Church of Jesus Christ of Latter-Day Saints—
Controversial literature.   2. Mormon Church—
Controversial literature.   3. Witness bearing
(Christianity)   I. Title.
BX8645.S65   1986   289.3   86-29828
ISBN 0-8007-9097-9

A Chosen Book
Copyright © 1986 by James R. Spencer

Chosen Books are published by
Fleming H. Revell Company
Old Tappan, New Jersey
Printed in the United States of America

This book is dedicated
to the victims of Mormonism.
To the victims,
really, of Joseph Smith,
an imaginative necromancer
who fell into something
bigger than even he could imagine.

Contents

Part 1: Initial Encounters

Chapter One
Talking to Mormons 15

Chapter Two
The Special Problems of Talking to Mormons 23

Chapter Three
Beginnings 34

Chapter Four
Preparing for the Encounter 44

Chapter Five
Opening the Dialogue .50

Chapter Six
Encountering the Three Mormon Types 56

Chapter Seven
Expanding the Encounter 69

Part 2: Encounters of the Best Kind

Chapter Eight
The Nature of God 77

Chapter Nine
Revelation 93

Chapter Ten
The Book of Mormon 112

Chapter Eleven
How to Answer Mormon Questions 129

Part 3: Advanced Encounters

Chapter Twelve
Some Topics You Should Understand 145

Chapter Thirteen
The Mormon Family 156

Chapter Fourteen
Encountering Mormon Salvation Theology 166

Part 4: Wisdom for Exiting Mormons

Chapter Fifteen
New Hope in Dealing with Mormonism 181

Chapter Sixteen
How to Resign from the Mormon Church 188

Appendix A: The Book of Mormon and the Nature
of God 195
Appendix B: Brigham H. Roberts: Mormon Giant Who
Lost Confidence in the Book of Mormon   197
Appendix C: Solomon Spalding's Manuscript and the
Book of Mormon 201
Appendix D: Psychological "Snapping" in the Cults . . 211
Resource Groups 213

Acknowledgments

My deepest appreciation to my wife, Margaretta, for helping me with the manuscript and for putting up with a man obsessed with what he thinks is a divine mission to rescue people (who, in most cases, don't want to be rescued) from the hell of religious oppression. I also thank Margaretta for the hours of proofreading and for her many useful suggestions.

I thank my congregation for their continued support of what is sometimes a controversial ministry.

Jim and Helen Close graciously provided a place—far from phones—for me to work.

I thank Jim Witham for his enthusiasm and editorial help.

I'm grateful to John Sherrill for his editorial suggestions.

And, last but not least, I thank those people who have touched my life with their zeal and love for those who are captive to the cults—people like Ed Decker, Walter Martin, Jerald and Sandra Tanner, Pat Matrisciana, Dave Hunt, Jo hanna Michaelson, Hal Lindsey, Bob Larson, and John Ankerberg. Some of these have touched me personally, others I know only through their work, which is surely engraved in golden libraries in heaven.

Author's Note

Since I wrote the story of my own involvement in Mormonism (*Beyond Mormonism: An Elder's Story*), I have received thousands of letters from all over the world. Many of them are from Mormons who write to say how the book has helped them sever the myriad gossamer threads of unholy doctrine.

I feel somewhat self-conscious sharing the private thoughts of these correspondents, which some will see as self-serving—a sales pitch for my earlier book.

But I want (and I'm sure those who wrote me share the same desire) to show the readers of this book how desperate and lonely their neighbors can be. Desperate for a listening ear—for someone who will understand and who will pray.

The hope of these letters is that Mormons *are* being touched with the message of a Christ who loves, accepts, and forgives them.

Part 1

Initial Encounters

Chapter One

Talking to Mormons

"The one thing I would tell anyone contemplating joining the Mormon Church is that it is so easy to join, but it is a literal, physical and mental hell to get out."

Keith

The orthodontist is young, good-looking, and successful. His office is dazzlingly clean with six patient's chairs in a row overlooking a groomed courtyard. His appointment calendar is set up in fifteen-minute intervals. He moves deftly from chair to chair adjusting crooked little smiles as nervous mothers wait in the wings.

In the consultation room he explains to my wife and me how our $2,600.00 will be spent on our daughter's teeth. Glancing at the written form on the table, he says, "Oh, I see you are a preacher."

"That's right," I respond. "I guess you're LDS, doctor?"

Smiling apologetically, the doctor says, "Well, I'm not a very *good* Mormon. I was as a kid, but . . . I don't know. . . ."

I am well-acquainted with this sheepish, I'm-sorry-I'm-not-a-good-Mormon routine. I have witnessed it frequently in "cultural" Mormons, Latter-day Saints who, for various reasons, are not "into" the Church.

"Someday I'll get active in the Church, but right now. . . ." His voice trails off.

"Well," I say, attempting to establish common ground and make him feel at ease, "people express their faith in various ways."

He rallies, "Yeah, that's where I am. I'm really a nice guy. I mean, I'm very tender. I cry at all the right places in the movies."

"You look like a sensitive person. I'm sure you think about spiritual things."

"I do! Not that I'm *terrifically* spiritual, but I have thoughts on the subject."

I haven't come to the dental appointment to witness to the orthodontist—I am there to conduct more mundane business. But as the conversation develops it becomes apparent that God has something more in mind. Out of the corner of my eye I see Margaretta picking up the drift of the conversation. I think I see her settle back into her chair. With minor trepidation I ask, "Dr. Nelson, you're a sensitive person who has serious thoughts about God. Do you mind if I ask you a personal question?"

"Well . . . I guess not."

"If I hear you right, you sort of find yourself alienated from your religious roots. I mean, you *are* a Latter-day Saint, but you are not active and you feel a little guilty about it."

"Yes, I guess that's true . . . but I view it as a temporary alienation."

"I understand," I continue, "but I also sense that you think the problem is your fault. I mean, the fact that you are not an active Mormon is due to some shortcoming within yourself?"

"Oh, I *know* it's my problem."

"Okay, wait a minute. I hear you, but I'm not sure I agree with you."

He eyes me curiously. "What do you mean?"

"Did you ever think that maybe it's not you who has the problem?"

The question takes him off guard. He focuses his attention on me. He understands that I am referring to his church. I figure he will become defensive and avoid this conversation. Instead, he merely continues to stare at me. The X-rays lie in a pile on the table between us. The whir of the air conditioning is the only sound in the room. Margaretta is listening intently. "Go ahead," he finally says quietly.

"Well, think about it," I plunge on. "You've assumed that because you don't fit in Mormonism, that something is wrong with you. Maybe that isn't true. Maybe you know something other Mormons don't. Is it possible that you sense something alien to you in Mormonism? Something that prevents you from fitting in? Maybe you don't fit with Mormonism because something is wrong with the system."

"Oh, I don't see how. . . ."

"I'm sure you wonder how that could be true. How could you know something that the Elders don't. After all, who are you."

Silence. I have the feeling he has asked these same questions of himself. I sense the struggle within him. "I mean, Mormonism is not the only religion in the world. In fact, in perspective, it's a rather minor religion. For every Mormon, for example, there are a hundred Roman Catholics. Just because you don't fit in doesn't necessarily mean you're wrong."

I'm sure the man has never had a conversation like this before. He's *thought* things about his faith that couldn't be spoken, but, suddenly, in an apparently inopportune moment, he finds himself in an intensely personal conversation. I know it's uncomfortable for him. And I know he has a choice to make. He can terminate the conversation with a word. Or he can choose to give me some more space.

As I wait for him to respond, I am once again overwhelmed by the complexity of trying to witness to a Mormon. This orthodontist is one of thousands of bright Mormons who walk around secretly alienated from their faith and unable to talk to anyone about it. Most Mormons

will never in a lifetime have a personal encounter with
someone who will share a genuine Gospel witness.

The dentist has been raised in what he has been taught
is the One True Church. He has attended Mormon grade
schools and a Mormon college. Until he opened his practice
he had belonged to the Church because of family and peer
pressure. And now he finds himself isolated: uninterested in
the Mormonism of his childhood, afraid to investigate anything else.

But he knows it's his problem. The Mormon Church is
true! Anybody who questions that is on the way to apostasy.
He's heard the apostasy stories since childhood: "Those who
doubt start down the road to apostasy and eventually end in
shipwreck." My Mormon friend entertains the idea that at
some time in the indefinite future he will return to the Mormon Church in full activity.

I understand how he feels. I myself once was an active
Mormon. I was a temple Mormon—that is, a Mormon ini-
tiated into the secret rites of the temple. I was a tithing Mormon who taught gospel doctrine classes and served the
Church wholeheartedly for years. I had been on a religious
treadmill, marching to the Elders' drumbeat, until God rescued me.

As I look into the eyes of this intelligent young man, I
marvel again at the power of deception. I am reminded of
what Ted DeMoss, who specializes in evangelizing business-
men, says: "The unsaved business or professional person is
not Gospel-*hardened;* he is Gospel-*ignorant.*" My dentist,
rather than being inured to the simple Gospel message, has
simply never heard it. "Dr. Nelson," I say, drawing a breath,
"can I tell you something very important?"

I quickly relate how much my personal relationship with
Jesus Christ means to me. I promise to send him a book and
he promises to read it. We return to the discussion of my
daughter's misaligned bite, and sometime later I am able to
share, in detail, the message of Christ.

Why Talk to Mormons?

Mormons have an enviable reputation for being so solid, so sure of their position, that they hold all of the initiative in any missionary effort. But is that really an accurate appraisal?

Mormonism is not the largest Church in the country, but it is one of the most visible and it is growing rapidly. A vibrant public relations campaign incorporates national television, magazines, radio, and newspapers to project an image of wholesome Mormon family life to America. Even though, for the most part, Americans accept their Mormon neighbors, or at least tolerate their religion, there is still some public reservation toward Mormonism: Utah is a strange land of temples and prophets, where one sees T-shirts bearing the message, "You are now in Utah: Turn your clock back 20 years."

Evangelical Christian leaders have watched Mormonism with dismay over the years, sometimes overwhelmed and intimidated, especially in the heartland sanctuary of the Rocky Mountains where Mormon authority has ruled unchallenged for 130 years. But until recently, outside the shelter of Utah proper, Mormondom has remained more of a theoretical than an actual problem for evangelical Christianity.

Today, however, Utah is no longer isolated from the rest of America. Suddenly, Mormonism is next door to everyone. Twentieth-century transportation, communications, and social mobility have sent Mormons throughout the country to live, work, and build churches, which means that evangelicals are in direct contact with Mormon missionaries coming out of Utah. At the same time the population tide has backed up from California, and evangelicals are moving into Utah. As evangelicals and Mormons find themselves eyeball-to-eyeball, both are startled but fascinated—the Zion Curtain has cracked!

Meanwhile, something else is happening. As the Utah frontiers break down, unexpected internal problems are shaking the Church to its foundations: Newly discovered historical documents are causing Mormon scholars to question the roots of Mormonism; the Book of Mormon is under attack from anthropologists at Brigham Young University (BYU) itself. The patriarchal authoritarianism of the elders is being challenged. As a result, I talk to exiting Mormons every week.

As pressures mount from within and without the Church, many Latter-day Saints are reexamining their faith. Today, before I sat down to write this, I spent four hours talking to three different Mormons who are leaving the Church.

It is my personal opinion (an opinion shared by many Mormon-watchers) that cataclysmic upheavals in Mormonism will cause tens of thousands of Mormons to exit the Church in the next few years. Many of these Mormons will be open to evangelization by Bible-believing Christians. This is the time to share the Gospel of Jesus Christ with Mormons.

Right Attitudes

For the most part, I think we Christians tend to make two mistakes with our Mormon friends: We are either too hard on them, or we fail to confront them honestly. If we are going to reach Latter-day Saints, we must follow the admonition of Paul, "speaking the truth in love" (Ephesians 4:15). Our watchword could well be: Truth without love is too hard; love without truth is too soft.

Some view Mormons as "the enemy." They approach Mormons in anger and fail to understand that they are victims of an oppressive religious system. Victims need love, understanding, and patience as well as truth. But, with "truth on our side," well-meaning evangelists charge into the battle, indiscriminately lopping off heads, forgetting that the cultist is to be won, not killed.

On the other hand, some people are so "loving" they forget to temper their acceptance with truth. To avoid being hard and arrogant they mistakenly fail to share the doctrinal minimum of orthodoxy. They don't want to be "negative." But it isn't negative to tell someone the painful truth—it's really very loving to do so. True love confronts. I can't avoid telling my neighbor his house is on fire simply because I don't want to be negative. A doctor cannot fail to treat a cancer because the treatment will upset and frighten the patient.

Fortunately, we don't have to settle for either of the extremes. It is possible to be truthful as well as loving. To be bold and sensitive, tough and tender. In order to do so, we will need to take inventory of our attitudes, prepare ourselves for battle, and pray for direction.

As a former Mormon Elder, a gospel doctrine teacher and one who has friends and relatives still in Mormonism, I have a special interest in seeing an effective evangelical approach directed toward Latter-day Saints.

Wherever I go to speak on the subject of Mormonism, I am asked one question more than any other: "How do I witness to my Mormon friends and relatives?"

That is not an easy question to answer. If three proof texts and a tract would convert Mormons, there would be no Mormonism. No, our task is not an easy one, but it is a *possible* one. And, if there is no one-two punch, there is, at least, a right approach to our Mormon friends. There are right and wrong things to do.

I do not attempt, in this book, to develop a specific step-by-step system of evangelizing Mormons; rather, I attempt to present a working philosophy for speaking to Mormons. I want you to understand the foundational errors of Mormonism so that you can relate to and empathize with Latter-day Saints.

In addition, I see this as a handbook to which you can refer to get specific help in specific areas. I will share information on subjects that invariably come up in conversation with Mormons. I will recommend subject areas to pursue as well as ones to avoid. I will share techniques (tactics) as well as philosophy (strategy).

My ideas about witnessing to my dearly beloved Mormon friends and neighbors are built on hundreds of hours of conversations with Mormons, former Mormons, and people who minister to Mormons.

My motive in witnessing to Mormons is that they may come into the same freedom I myself have experienced in Christ.

Chapter Two

The Special Problems of Talking to Mormons

"I picked up a copy of your book in a Christian bookstore that I frequent. I must admit that I bought your book in order to study what you were saying about the Church and understand why you had left it [so I would be] better equipped to disprove what you were teaching.... Instead what you wrote just made me desire to learn more....

"I just want to let you know that there are those that you do reach.... There are still a lot of questions that go through my mind but ... I want you to know that I have received salvation."

Bruce

Joseph Smith, the founder of Mormonism, said men live on the moon. Why he said that, no one knows, but he did. He said the moon-dwellers were about six feet tall, dressed like Quakers, and lived to be a thousand years old.[1]

Of course no one believes that today. Well, almost no one. My friend Bob Bryant had a conversation with an otherwise intelligent engineer who found a way to believe in Smith's "moon people."

Bob and the engineer were discussing the prophecies of

1. *The Young Woman's Journal,* "The Inhabitants of the Moon," 1892, Vol. 3, p. 263.

Joseph Smith. Bob mentioned several of Smith's odd prophecies that did not come to pass—including the prophecy that
we would find inhabitants on the moon. Bob said, "Look,
we've been to the moon. We've sent astronauts there. There
are no tall Quakers."

The engineer had to admit that it looked like Joseph Smith
had been wrong on that one. But, a few days later, approaching Bob tentatively, he reopened the conversation. "I
know you're not going to like this," he said. "But I've been
thinking—maybe the men Joseph Smith talked about live
under the surface of the moon. He may yet be vindicated."

Bob swears the guy was serious. And I believe it, because I
have had dozens of similar conversations with Latter-day
Saints who were otherwise reasonable, but who became ir-
rational when it came to their faith.

How, you ask, can a bright, educated person swallow
something like that? How can he be so dedicated to a system
that he is willing to believe almost *anything?*

I asked that question of Dr. Walter Martin, a man known
throughout the world as a foremost authority on cults. Dr.
Martin is the author of *The Kingdom of the Cults* and *The
Maze of Mormonism*. We met at a terrace coffee shop overlooking the golf course at Elkhorn in Sun Valley, Idaho,
where we were both addressing a convention on Mormon-
sim.

"Jim," Dr. Martin said with characteristic enthusiasm,
"the problem is that Mormonism has altered the *thinking
process* of Mormons in the area of religion! A Mormon can
think very rationally about his job, what clothes to wear,
and things like that, but when you push the button on religion he stops thinking and gives you what he has been
taught."

"You mean he fails to think reasonably about his spiritual
life?"

"That's it exactly."

I told Dr. Martin that his observation confirmed my own

experience with Latter-day Saints. "It's almost as though they are blind in the area of the spirit."

"It's worse than that. They have given up their right to think independently. They cannot *hear* spiritually. Paul said, 'If our gospel is hid, it is hid because the god of this world has blinded their minds.' "

The "god of this world" is Satan. Interesting. Sipping coffee on a sun deck in Sun Valley with Dr. Martin, watching swallows sweep out across the golf course, the idea of Satan deceiving millions of people seemed like a distant thunder. Soon I would be returning to the workaday world of pastoring in Mormondom. I knew from personal experience the frustration of dealing with a people who totally and blindly submit to Church hierarchy.

I thought of a young girl I had recently spoken to. I asked her to explain why the Book of Mormon states that Jesus was born at Jerusalem, when historically He was born in Bethlehem. She, of course, did not believe it said that. I was at a crucial turning point with her because most Mormons consider the Book of Mormon to be infallible. I remembered the fear in her eyes when I showed the passage to her in her own Book of Mormon.[2] She was shaken and perplexed.

But a few days later when I saw her, she was again full of confidence. "I talked to my bishop about that Book of Mormon passage," she said.

"Great," I replied. "What did he say?"

"Well," she said, "Jesus was born in Bethlehem—the bishop admits that. But because Bethlehem is only twelve miles from Jerusalem, it's technically okay to say He was born *at* Jerusalem."

Dr. Martin interrupted my reflection. "Talking about spiritual things to Mormons," he said, "is like trying to describe a rainbow to a blind man. You are talking about a rainbow to a guy who doesn't know what color is."

2. Alma 7:10.

I think the biggest hurdle for the evangelical Church is to get past the idea that Mormons are Protestants who simply have some doctrinal problems. Nothing could be further from the truth. Mormonism is a religious system that stands in direct opposition to basic teachings of the Bible. For example, Mormonism teaches:

—Jesus Christ is the "spirit brother" of Satan.[3]

—Jesus was conceived as the result of physical sex between God the Father and the Virgin Mary; He was *not* conceived by the Holy Ghost.[4]

—The wedding in Cana was the wedding of none other than Jesus Himself, who wed three women: Mary, her sister Martha, and "the other Mary." And He had children by them.[5]

—Every worthy member of the Mormon Church can become a god—just like God Himself. In fact, Mormons teach that God was once a man, who "progressed to godhood."[6] One Mormon authority recently published a widely received book in which he declared that God could "cease to be God" if He lost the support of the *other* gods.[7]

—The doctrines of the holy Trinity and salvation by grace are, in the words of Mormon apostle Bruce R. McConkie, "the two Great Heresies of Christendom."[8] That same apostle, in a speech at Brigham Young University, warned students that striving for "a special personal relationship with Christ is both improper and perilous."[9]

3. Bruce R. McConkie, *Mormon Doctrine*, Bookcraft, Salt Lake City, 1979, pp. 193, 589–590, 751.
4. *Journal of Discourses*, The Church of Jesus Christ of Latter-day Saints, 1966, Vol. 1, pp. 50–51.
5. *Journal of Discourses*, Vol. 4, pp. 259–260; Vol. 1, 345–346.
6. McConkie, pp. 238–239; *Journal of Discourses*, Vol. 6, p. 3.
7. W. Cleon Skousen, *The First 2,000 Years*, Bookcraft, pp. 355–356.
8. Speech at Brigham Young University, Jan. 10, 1984.
9. Speech at Brigham Young University, March 2, 1982.

Life in the Church/State

Mormonism advertises the virtues of Mormon family life, refusing to look at the facts about deteriorating Mormon society. For example, Utah, which is 67% Mormon, records divorce rates, child abuse rates, teen suicide rates, rape rates, and child homicide rates consistently *higher* than the national average.[10]

The Mormon Church wields remarkable power over its membership, especially in the heartland of Mormondom where it owns both of Salt Lake City's daily newspapers, the largest TV and radio stations, most of the downtown real es-

10. —Salt Lake City has twice the number of rapes as other cities its size (*Los Angeles Times*, June 26, 1983, Part I, p. 25).

—20% of all murder victims in Utah are under the age of 15—five times the national average (*Salt Lake Tribune*, Aug. 13, 1982).

—Authorities have dubbed Utah "The fraud capitol of the world." U.S. Attorney Brent Ward says 10,000 investors lost $200 million between 1980–1982 in Utah-connected frauds (*Salt Lake Tribune*, "Swindlers Find Utah Easy Prey," Aug. 25, 1985).

—The divorce rate in Utah is consistently higher than the national average (*World Almanac*, 1986, pp. 261, 779).

—According to the National Center for Health Statistics, Utah marriages last only two-thirds as long as those of the nation as a whole. And the most common age for women to divorce in Utah is age 20 (*Denver Post*, "Utah: Inside the Church State," Nov. 20–28, 1982, Special Report, p. 10).

—Forty percent of all women marry in their teens in Utah and of those who have children in their teens, two thirds are pregnant out of wedlock (*Los Angeles Times*, June 26, 1983, Part I. p. 25).

—Teen suicide in Utah is 20% higher than the national average (*Salt Lake Tribune*, "Suicide Among Utah Teens Continues Grim Climb," July 8, 1985, p. 8B).

—Utah is the 34th most populous state, but ranks 13th in child abuse in the nation (*Salt Lake Tribune*, "Child Abuse on Rise in Predominately Mormon Utah," June 26, 1982, p. 6A).

tate, and the biggest retail department store. The Mormon Church also owns Utah's largest life insurance company, has interests in railroads and sugar refineries, and it takes in more than $3 million a day.[11] And a Mormon's life is no less regulated outside Utah. At one time or another, Mormon volunteer laborers have manned Church-owned farms in the Midwest, canneries on the West Coast, a 300,000-acre cattle ranch in Florida, a peanut butter factory in Texas, and an apartment complex in New York.[12]

In Utah, the Mormon Church controls the state legislature and dominates nearly every municipal government. All of Utah's U.S. Congressmen are Mormons.

The Revelation Question

Mormonism is rooted in what it calls "The Restoration"— the idea that all spiritual authority was lost from the earth with the death of the last apostle in the first century. God "restored" the Church of Christ through Joseph Smith. Joseph was led to gold plates by an angel named Moroni, and translated the plates "by the gift and power of God" into the Book of Mormon.

Yet such restoration is apparently never final in Mormonism. God seems to change His mind on issues such as polygamy and priesthood. For, in spite of the views of such modern Mormon authorities as Ezra Taft Benson that it is "the most correct book on earth,"[13] the Book of Mormon has been heavily edited since it was first published in 1830.

Mormons believe that God inspired the Bible, and accord-

11. For the latest and most comprehensive study of Mormon financial structure, see *The Mormon Corporate Empire,* John Heinerman and Anson Shupe, Beacon Press, Boston, 1985.
12. See Footnote 11.
13. *Idaho Falls Post Register,* "Christ in Christmas, Prophet Says," Dec. 2, 1985.

ing to the Eighth Article of Faith it is the Word of God, "insofar as it is translated correctly."

In other words, God inspired the Bible but He did not preserve it. The Book of Mormon and other Latter-day scripture exists to restore "the many plain and precious truths which have been lost from the Bible."

High-ranking Mormons can speak the "Word of the Living Prophet" and such utterance is as binding as Scripture. Brigham Young said, "I have never preached a sermon and sent it out to the children of men, that they cannot call Scripture. Let me have a privilege of correcting a sermon, and it's as good a Scripture as they deserve."[14]

So Mormonism claims, as the Church of the Restoration, to be God's answer to what it sees as confusion among the denominations. Mormonism, however, clarifies nothing. It is, in fact, extremely complicated and confusing. It is full of change and paradox. For example:

—The Book of Mormon has been changed in nearly 4,000 places since it was published 150 years ago.[15]

—The Book of Abraham, which Joseph Smith said was "the writings of Abraham while he was in Egypt," is in fact an Egyptian funeral text.[16]

—The Church instituted polygamy as a "new and everlasting covenant" and repeatedly swore it should never give the doctrine up. But, in 1890, when the United States government threatened to confiscate the holdings of the Church in Utah and banish Mormonism to Mexico, "suddenly" God

14. For Brigham Young's statement see *Journal of Discourses*, Vol. 13, p. 95. Ezra Taft Benson shocked Mormon liberals in his 1980 speech when he said, "The Prophet does not have to say, 'Thus sayeth the Lord' to give us scripture." ("Fourteen Fundamentals in Following the Prophets," BYU Devotional Assembly, Feb. 26, 1980.)
15. See Chapter Ten.
16. Jerald and Sandra Tanner, *Mormonism—Shadow or Reality?*, "Fall of the Book of Abraham," Utah Lighthouse Ministry, Salt Lake City, pp. 294–369, Fourth edition, 1982.

produced a "new revelation" and the Church abandoned the practice.[17]

—For 140 years the Church would not let blacks hold the Mormon priesthood, but during the civil rights activism of the 1960s, when the Church's General Conferences began to be picketed by civil rights groups, President Spencer W. Kimball "got a revelation" that the blacks were now to be allowed to hold the priesthood. Shortly after that, the Book of Mormon was again edited to reflect the change.

A Packaged Religion

People who are interested in Mormonism are told to pray about the legitimacy of a whole package of authority—sources that include Joseph Smith, the Book of Mormon, the current Prophet, and the Mormon Church. The faithful Mormon fails to differentiate between God and the Church It will be a source of wonder to him that you are able to do so.

Mormon converts are required to forfeit their right to question authority. They are told to trust the "feeling" they get in response to their investigative prayer. Once they make that purely subjective determination (called their "testimony"), they have found "The Truth." They are to believe whatever they are told from that point.

Eventually (but never immediately) the Mormon convert will be asked to believe in polytheism, polygamy, and bizarre temple ceremonies such as symbolically slitting one's own throat for faithlessness. When they question these things, they question their entire commitment to the Church. Once they have "their testimony" they are taught to trust that subjective experience in the face of all logic and reason. Each month a "fast and testimony" meeting is held for Mormons to gather together to reinforce their commitment to the

17. *Doctrine and Covenants*, Official Declaration No. 1.

Church by publicly declaring their allegiance to the Church and the Prophet.[18]

Foundations of Fear

We must never forget that Mormons themselves are victims of a system and organization—a *church*. Until we realize how much of a delusion Mormonism is, we will not have the reservoir of patience required to deal with our Latter-day Saint friends.

We need to know how deeply the intimidation of Mormonism goes. Christians who have never experienced the bondage of a cult system cannot easily realize what these people are up against.

Since I wrote my first book on this subject, *Beyond Mormonism: An Elder's Story,* I have received thousands of letters and phone calls from Mormons. One common denominator runs through all the conversations: *fear.* Black, sticky fear. Paralyzing fear. Mormons who want out can't get out. Those who choose to brave the odds and leave their Church often pay heavy prices. Some lose their families.

I wonder that any escape. In fact, without a great undertaking of grace, they would not escape. But they do, often with brilliant displays of courage:

—A thirteen-year-old girl from Murray, Utah, wrote me to say that she had accepted Christ three-and-a-half months earlier. Her parents are "twice-a-week" temple Mormons. "The tension is building very quickly in our home," she

18. Some Mormons attempt to compare the Mormon conversion experience to the decision Christians make to trust Jesus Christ as Savior and Lord. But that is not a legitimate comparison. A person who relinquishes control to God is in an entirely different position from one who gives up his control to a system or a person or a church. No legitimate Christian worker will attempt to convince someone to submit his destiny to a denomination, group, or prophet.

wrote. She added, "Even if I have to lose my family [for Christ] it will be worth it."

—A 74-year-old woman from Kansas, after she and her husband made the decision to leave the Mormon Church, wrote: "Home teachers are still coming. We wish they would not. . . . They tell us they are commanded to come. . . . Could you tell us what excommunication is [like]? We don't want to have to explain to a bunch of elders. . . . Please—what is our next step?"

—A Mormon woman from Texas said since she has been born again, she has experienced many abuses from the Mormon Church. And she has suffered at the hands of her husband who is a Stake Missions President. "They tell me I am a follower of Satan and threaten me. My husband has hit me a number of times and left bruises. I can't get far enough from the Church to 'get well' or recover from being brainwashed. . . . Can you please, please be my friend?"

—A few days ago I received a letter from a young airman stationed in Maine. He is a Mormon who is struggling with his faith. Something is lacking, but he doesn't know what it is. He sneaked into a Baptist church one evening where he saw a magazine with my testimony in it. He wrote me full of questions. He opened his letter fearfully: "I'm confused and upset. . . . I am afraid to write to you, but the Spirit says, 'Do not be afraid.' . . . Do not send anyone to see me, please. I am afraid. But you can send me a letter. . . . Writing to you has been one of the hardest things I have ever done . . . I can't talk to *anyone*."

I didn't urge him to leave Mormonism. I urged him to get to know Jesus Christ. To read the Bible. To visit an evangelical church. I asked him to risk talking to a Christian pastor.

A Call to Compassion

I don't get impatient with my Mormon friends who struggle with the stickiness of escaping Mormonism. Rather,

I weep for them and pray for them. I realize that "our struggle is not against flesh and blood, but against the rulers,
against the authorities, against the powers of this dark world
and against the spiritual forces of evil in the heavenly
realms." (See Ephesians 6:12.)

The first step to helping Mormons is to come to terms with
the fact that Mormonism is a system hatched in hell and
birthed in the occult necromancies of Joseph Smith. The
next chapter of this book documents the dark beginnings of
Mormonism. This is a discussion that is not pleasant, but is
necessary. Mormonism makes it necessary. Hilary, Bishop
of Poitiers, said in the fourth century that the errors of the
heretics force us to discuss repugnant things.[19] Jude said he
would prefer to speak of our common faith, but he was
"compelled" to contend for the accuracy of the faith (see Jude 3).

I want you to know how Mormons think. What they feel.
How they have come to the doctrinal abyss of Mormonism.

Knowing what you are up against will give you the foundation for deciding if you are willing to pay the sacrificial
price of loving Mormons.

I think you can do it.

And I believe you will be motivated for the task by prepa-
ration. Knowledge is a source of enthusiasm.

There is, within Latter-day Saints I meet, a growing hun-
ger. A cry for deliverance.

God has heard their cry.

Perhaps you will be the instrument He will use to bring a
Mormon soul to Jesus Christ.

19.   *On the Trinity,* 2.2, cited in Harold O.J. Brown, *Heresies,* Doubleday
      and Company, 1984, p. xx.

Chapter Three

Beginnings

"I was given your book to read and it has really touched me. After much agonizing for several months, I have accepted the grace of Christ as totally sufficient for my relationship with my heavenly Father. . . .

"For a while I continued active in the LDS Ward and attended Protestant Bible classes. Now that I am saved I realize the hopeless irreconcilable differences between Christ's grace and the total emphasis on self-perfection at the LDS Church. I value my new understanding so much I cannot jeopardize it by hearing the opposite anymore."

Delia

Mitch Belobaba leaned his chair against my file cabinets sipped a glass of water. The small fan only stirred the heat in my cramped office. He was wearing a khaki shirt shorts. A floppy hat was folded and tucked into his belt

Mitch, on furlough from his duties as an evangelical r sionary to Africa, had just driven to our church from family home in Vancouver, B.C. He was to speak to us evening about the condition of missions in Africa and rope. Mitch is intelligent, animated, and tireless. But this ternoon he looked fatigued and troubled.

"I'm perplexed, Jim," he said. "I need some info."

"Sure, Mitch, what is it?"

"Well, as you know, I've been on the road for the last three months, touring the United States."

"Yeah, it must get tiring. . . ."

"It does, but that isn't what's bothering me. My problem began two weeks ago when I first came to this area. As you know, I drove from Omaha to a church in Pocatello, Idaho. Then I went home to Vancouver for ten days, and now I'm back, continuing my speaking schedule."

"You explained that in your letter."

"What I didn't explain is what happened to me two weeks ago. It's very strange . . . I need to talk to somebody about it."

I was flattered that he would think I could help him.

"I had been driving pretty hard for a couple of days when I arrived in Kemmerer, Wyoming," Mitch continued. "When I got to Kemmerer, I was suddenly overcome with the strangest feeling. It was eerie. I thought maybe God was trying to say something to me. The last time I experienced anything like it was when my daughter was seriously ill and I was away from home."

Mitch mopped the perspiration from his brow. "So I called home."

"And?"

"Nothing, everything was all right. So I wrote it off as fatigue. But I was disturbed for two days. The feeling never left.

"When I finished my presentation in Pocatello, I drove home. The funny thing is that when I reached Twin Falls, just two hours west of Pocatello, the feeling lifted."

I felt a chill and the hair stood up on my arms. I knew what he was going to say next. I interrupted him. "Wait a minute, Mitch," I said slowly, "let me finish the story."

He stopped short and looked blankly at me.

"When you drove back here," I said evenly, "you felt it start again when you passed Twin Falls coming east."

Now it was Mitch's turn to shudder. "That's right! But, how did—"

"Lean forward, brother," I said. "I need to get into that file cabinet."

I placed a manila envelope on the desk in front of him. He looked at me for a few seconds, then opened it and inspected the acetate overhead projector sheet inside.

Mitch whistled softly. "Wow!"

What he saw on the overhead sheet was a map of the western United States. On the map I had delineated "Mormondom," the Latter-day Saint Kingdom that spills over from Utah into Wyoming, Idaho, Colorado, Nevada, Arizona, and California. *A marking pencil line passed through the town of Kemmerer, on the east, and just inside Twin Falls, on the west.*

"Of course," Mitch said. "Mormonism! I should have known. I should have figured this out before. But I didn't expect to see it here ... in this country. This is the same oppressive spirit I encounter in Africa."

Mitch's reaction was not new to me. Every evangelist seems to experience the same shock when first encountering Mormondom. One evangelist described landing at Idaho Falls airport as a "descent into darkness." Another, Lowell Lundstrom, who has traveled the western United States for 25 years, told me of his first trip to Mormondom. As his big Greyhound bus descended the rockies from Montana into Eastern Idaho, he said, "We drove into some kind of dark spiritual soup."

What is the background of this strange religion?

Mormon Roots

Mormonism was born in western New York at the beginning of the nineteenth century—a time of excitement and vision following the Revolutionary War, when those of pioneer spirit drove the boundaries of the nation west. Pioneers and preachers, traders and opportunists, politicians, and dreamers rode riverboats and barges to points west along the Erie Canal, which flowed only a few hundred feet from young Joseph Smith's hometown, Palmyra.

It was an era of adventure and experimentation—both political and religious. The frontier was referred to as "the psychic highway" and looked upon by orthodox churchmen as a hotbed of "ultraism" where settlers brought with them an experimental approach to relogous and social ideas. The times produced, as well as Mormonism, such movements as Shakerism, spiritualism, and the sexual communism of the Oneida Community. Thomas Paine argued for skepticism and John Murray for Universal Salvation. It was an age of fervor and fanaticism. An age of religious innovators or "seekers," who in reaction to established religion drafted their faith from the pages of the Bible (and sometimes from other documents).

The hot pursuit of religious experience in brush arbors and revivals occurred with such frequency that the Presbyterian evangelist Charles Finney referred to the area as the "burnt-over district." It was a time when a charismatic preacher could gather followers to new and revolutionary ideas. On the frontier, a man's education was not as important as his persuasiveness.

This then was the mood of the area where the Smith family settled. The surge of pioneer activity had carried the Smiths to western New York with the hope of acquiring farmland. The Smith family was a product of its environment. They moved to Palmyra, New York, in 1816 from Vermont, when Joseph was eleven years old. Joseph's paternal grandfather was a Universalist and his maternal grandfather "had no religion" until the age of seventy-five. Joseph's mother and father had started married life with a "handsome" four-year-old farm and $1,000, but bad business decisions had reduced them to poverty by the time they reached Palmyra in 1816. They arrived in town with "a small wagon-load of possessions and 9 cents in cash."[1]

Joseph Smith was, without doubt, most influenced by his mother, Lucy Mack Smith. Lucy was a strong-willed woman born on the eighth of July, 1775. In her biography of her son, published after his death, she said she mainly remembered "illness and death" in her own childhood. Lucy was opinionated, vindictive, and given to a morose spirit.

Lucy spent a lifetime seeking but never finding peace with God. Preacher after preacher explained the way of salvation, but she could not accept the explanations. She was openly critical of those men of God she encountered. One preacher she rejected because he "neither understood nor appreciated the subject upon which he spoke." Likewise, her husband, although often attracted to the evangelical message, concluded that religionists generally "knew nothing about the Kingdom of God." Lucy eventually decided "there was not, upon the face of the earth, the religion she sought."

Like his parents, young Joseph could not find peace with God. His mother wrote that he said he "wanted to get religion too, to feel and shout like the rest, but he could feel nothing."

Joseph was inquisitive, good-natured, and uneducated. Because of the extreme poverty of the Smith family, father and son together hired out to various farmers to mend fences, dig wells, and help cultivate their neighbors' land.

The Smiths were gullible. Without inoculation against the superstitions of frontier life, it is not surprising that they began to dabble in the world of the occult. Water-witching and treasure-seeking by way of mysterious "seer-stones" were practiced by uneducated residents of the frontier. Rumors circulated that pirates and "Spaniards" had hidden

1.   Richard Bushman, *Joseph Smith and the Beginnings of Mormonism,*
     University of Illinois Press, Chicago, 1984, p. 42.

gold and silver in the hills around Palmyra. The whole Smith clan spent hours seeking treasure to end their impoverishment.

It is historical fact that Joseph Smith hired out to dig for treasure. March 20, 1826, when Joseph was twenty years old, he was convicted for being a "disorderly person" and "an imposter," the charges stemming from his apparently illegal practice of divining with a "seer-stone." An original court document, found in 1971, states that Joseph was convicted of the still-illegal practice of witchcraft as a "glass-looker." Testimony in the trial relates that Joseph professed that by looking through a "peep-stone," he could divine the location of buried treasure, gold mines, and kettles of coined gold and silver.

It was in the context of treasure-seeking that Joseph Smith first began to speak of finding "gold plates." Shortly after he published the Book of Mormon in 1830, his hometown newspaper, *The Palmyra Reflector,* published this account:

> It is well known that Jo Smith never pretended to have any communion with angels, until long after the PRE-TENDED finding of his book ... and it is equally well known that a vagabond fortune-teller by the name of Walters ... was the constant companion and bosom friend of these money digging imposters. ... There remains little doubt ... that Walters ... suggested to Smith the idea of finding a book. Walters ... had procured an old copy of Cicero's Orations, in the Latin language, out of which he would read long and loud to his credulous hearers, uttering at the same time an unintelligible jargon, which he would afterwards pretend to interpret and explain, as a record of the former inhabitants of America, and a particular account of the numerous situations where they deposited their treasures.[2]

2. *Palmyra Reflector*, Feb. 28, 1831, as cited in Jerald and Sandra Tanner, "Mormonism, Magic and Masonry," Utah Lighthouse Ministry, Salt Lake City, 1983, pp. 1–2.

Joseph Smith himself gained a reputation as a first-rate storyteller. His mother, in her biography of Joseph, told how he would entertain the family for hours, describing the lifestyle of the ancient Indian inhabitants of western New York: their government, wars, dress, all in painstaking detail. And this was *long before* he ever suggested getting such details from a visitation of angels.

As Joseph continued his practice of divination and storytelling, he befriended others equally anxious to find treasure. The family gave itself more and more to treasure-seeking to such an extent that Lucy defends the family's preoccupation with magic. She wrote:

> ... Let not the reader suppose that ... we stopt our labor and went about trying to win the faculty of Abrac, drawing magic circles, or sooth saying, to the neglect of all kinds of business. We never during our lives suffered one important interest to swallow up every other obligation.[3]

However, as time went on, the Smiths' excursions into the occult became more eccentric. The classic work, *Mormonism Unveiled,* published in 1834, contains an affidavit by a Peter Ingersoll who related how Joseph Smith, Sr., told him he had divined chests of gold and silver with a seer-stone. On one occasion, Ingersoll said, the elder Smith

> ... Put the stone ... into his hat, and stooping forward, he bowed and made sundry movements, quite similar to those of a stool pigeon. At length he took down his hat, and being very much exhausted, said, in a faint voice, 'If you knew what I had seen, you would believe.' ... His son Alvin (Joseph Smith, Jr.'s, oldest brother) then went through with the same performance, which was equally disgusting.[4]

3. *Joseph Smith's Bainbridge, New York, Court Trials,* Wesley Walters, Part 2, pp. 126–127, as cited in Tanner, *Mormonism, Magic and Masonry,* p. 20.
4. E.D. Howe, *Mormonism Unveiled,* Painesville, Ohio, 1834, pp. 232–233.

Young Joseph soon became the center of spiritual power in the family. He was the "gifted one." More and more he became the "prophet." And his activities became darker in their nature. A man named Joseph Capron testified to the occult nature of the Smiths' activities. He said young Joseph used stakes to form a circle around treasure, which he divined was buried on Capron's property. Evil spirits, Joseph claimed, had taken possession of a chest of gold watches buried northwest of Capron's house. Joseph ordered stakes to be driven in the ground around the spot where the treasure supposedly lay. He then sent a messenger to Palmyra to obtain a polished sword. While the treasure-seekers dug for the gold, another seer marched around the circle brandishing the sword. Alas, Capron reported, "in spite of their brave defense . . . the devil came off victorious, and carried away the watches."[5]

Under cover of darkness, swords and incantations and occult manipulations grew more radical and gruesome. William Stafford swore in an affidavit that Joseph used one of Stafford's black sheep as a blood sacrifice. After cutting the throat of the sheep, "it [was] led around a circle while bleeding" to appease "the wrath of the evil spirit . . . [so that] treasures could then be obtained." Cynically, Stafford concluded that while they didn't get the treasure, they probably ate the sheep. "This, I believe," he said, "is the only time they ever made money-digging a profitable business."[6]

Others testified that Joseph sacrificed lambs, roosters, and even a pet dog in his efforts to obtain treasure. He even viewed the murder of one of their company as a "providential occurrence."[7]

Joseph's necromancy mixed Bible reading and prophesy with occult manipulations. In fact, his Christian philosophy was being formulated at the same time his occult skills were

5. Howe, pp. 259–260.
6. Howe, pp. 237–239.
7. Tanner, *Mormonism, Magic and Masonry*, pp. 32–35.

being sharpened. He became convinced that mankind had missed its chance for salvation. That "there was no society or denomination that built upon the Gospel of Jesus Christ as recorded in the New Testament."[8]

His conversations with clergymen and others led him to the same dead end his mother faced. They had no answers for him. Neither would the Bible be sufficient to answer his questions. He said, in his own *History of the Church*, that there was no way of settling religious questions "by an appeal to the Bible."[9] If he were to learn anything about God, it would have to come from his own personal revelation. He wanted a manifestation that would lead him to ultimate truth. More and more he began to see his own spiritual gift as the only hope for finding that truth. Gradually, his family and a few others began to believe in him.

During this time Joseph received regular visitations from the spirit world. And though he would rewrite the official versions many times, eventually he would see this series of visions as the foundation for a new and radical religion. He would be the founder of the One True Church. All others were "wrong ... all their creeds were an abomination in [God's] sight ... [and all the professors of those creeds] were corrupt...."[10] The Truth had been taken from the earth and it was up to Joseph to restore it.

The visitations of the being who has come to be called "the angel Moroni" occurred over three successive years, always on or about the autumnal equinox. This "angelic being" was going to show Joseph buried gold plates, which would be translated into the Book of Mormon.

Joseph's visitations continued throughout his life and they form the basis of his claim to be "The Prophet." Ultimately

8. Bushman, p. 55.
9. *History of the Church,* Deseret Book Company, Salt Lake City, 1978, Vol. 1, pp. 3-4.
10. *Pearl of Great Price,* Joseph Smith 2:19.

Joseph would rewrite Christian doctrine, including the Bible, calling his own "The Inspired Version." He would lead his people into polytheism and polygamy. He would establish a communal kingdom at war with its neighbors. He would become wealthy, found a bank (which failed), and become a mayor, a general, and, finally, a candidate for the Presidency of the United States. Joseph met his death in an Illinois jail at the hands of an angry mob. As he died, he emptied a smuggled revolver into a crowd, killing two men.[11]

Of his own career, Joseph said, "No man ever did such a work as I."[12] Not Paul, John, Peter, or even Jesus!

"I combat the errors of ages," Joseph said. "I cut the Gordian knot of powers, and I solve the mathematical problems of universities, with truth—diamond truth; and *God is my 'right hand man.'* "[13]

11. *History of the Church*, Vol. 7, pp. 101–103 and Vol. 6, p. XLI.
12. *History of the Church*, Vol. 6, pp. 408–409.
13. *History of the Church*, Vol. 6, p. 78.

Chapter Four

Preparing for the Encounter

> "I, like your wife, was raised as a devout Mormon—attending all Church functions as a youngster, graduating from seminary classes while attending high school in Utah, and finally graduating from BYU.
>
> "I, like so many, was a disappointment (to myself and my family) when I married 'outside the Church.'
>
> "Your book has helped me to finally come to grips with the hidden feelings of failure I experienced when leaving the Church."
>
> **Elizabeth**

I recently received a pitiful letter from a Christian girl who had fallen in love with a Mormon—a "returned missionary." Julie had been raised in a Christian home, the daughter of an evangelical minister, but she hadn't been educated about Mormonism.

Julie's new boyfriend, Charles, was handsome, dedicated to his convictions, articulate. And he was leading her into Mormonism.

No one had inoculated Julie against Mormonism, because talking about someone else's faith is considered "negative." No one ever told Julie, for example, that Mormons (as we will see later) believe in the existence of many gods. Since no one had mentioned the pagan polytheism of Mormonism,

Julie had grown up regarding Mormonism as simply another denomination.

Charles, of course, was not about to bring up the subject of polytheism. Rather, as she wrote me, Charles "bore her his testimony" from "the bottom of his heart" with "every fiber of his being," believing that Joseph Smith was a True Prophet of God who restored the One True Church.

Charles told her how the Three Witnesses had sworn that they had seen the gold plates from which the Book of Mormon was translated. (He did not tell her that all three had been excommunicated from the Mormon Church after they lost confidence in Joseph Smith and accused him of lying, adultery, and "deep . . . error and blindness.")[1]

Nor did Charles mention occult temple ceremonies or that polygamy would be restored in heaven. He simply stressed the "wonderful Mormon family life" (which, as we will see, is not borne out by statistics) and led her through a series of often twisted proof texts about water baptism, priesthood, and prophecy.

It was a garden path for Julie.

Now she wrote me a tear-stained letter saying, "Everything I have believed is under attack. Mormonism seems so logical. And I can't think my way out. Can you *please* help me?"

Moved as I was by Julie's cry for help, unfortunately I could be of little help. She did not want to break away from Mormonism. By the time she wrote she was already convinced that Mormonism was "logical" and that it would be immature to continue to hold onto the faith of her childhood.

I read Julie's letter to my eighteen-year-old daughter. "Dad," Erin asked with anguish, "why was Julie so *uninformed?*" My daughter was frustrated that the young woman's family and church had sent her unprepared into a

---

1. *Elders' Journal*, August, 1838, p. 59, and David Whitmer, *An Address to All Believers in Christ*, Richmond, Missouri, 1887, pp. 27–28.

world full of cult missionaries. My daughter knew what Julie's parents apparently did not know: that by the time she came home asking questions, she was already neck-deep in doctrinal discussions.

I find it pitiful that the daughter of an evangelical pastor had to write a stranger to get elementary information about Mormonism.

An Hour of Decision

Julie didn't get training in Christian foundation thinking because our Christian society fails to recognize the attack of the cults. We do not fully understand the threat of the cults.[2]

Confronting cults is distasteful. Dealing with heresy has always been distasteful. But to fail to take appropriate action against heresy is an equally dangerous extreme. Consider:

—Jude said he would have preferred to write about Christians' common faith, but that he was constrained to "contend for the faith," because godless men had "slipped in among you" (Jude 3–4).

—Peter wrote of "false teachers among you ... [who would] introduce destructive heresies" (2 Peter 2:1–2).

—John said the spirit of antichrist would spring up from within the Christian Church. That men would rise up within Christianity and lead people out of the churches. "If they had belonged to us, they would have remained with us; but their going showed that none of them belonged to us" (1 John 2:19).

---

2.   Christian television networks (and some Christian magazines) are reluctant to object to Mormonism. Ed Decker, author of *The God Makers* and producer of the film by that title, was canceled on one of the major Christian TV networks recently because the owner felt "it would offend our Mormon partners."

—The apostle Paul called these men "savage wolves" who would spring up within the Church, men who would rise up and "distort the truth in order to draw away disciples" (Acts 20:29–31).

"Keep reminding" the people of orthodoxy, Paul said; "correctly handle the word of truth" and prevent the spread of nonsense. Of men like Hymenaeus and Philetus (who taught heresy about the Resurrection) he said, "Their teaching will spread like gangrene ... [and] destroy the faith of some" (2 Timothy 2:14–18).

"There are many rebellious people ... deceivers ... [who] must be silenced, because they are ruining whole households," he told Titus (Titus 1:10–11).

Those of us who encounter heresy do so not because we enjoy it, but because it is necessary. Hilary of Poitirs, writing in the fourth century, said:

> The errors of the heretics ... force us to deal with unlawful matters, to scale the perilous heights, to speak unutterable words, to trespass on forbidden ground.[3]

We need to wake up to the fact that we are in a war for souls. The Mormon Church fields *29,000* full-time missionaries (about as many as the *entire* evangelical Church) and these missionaries garner half to three-quarters of their converts from members of Christian churches.

Cults thrive because the Church of Christ allows them to do business without intellectual challenge. We march with determination toward the Promised Land, "while the Devil takes the hindmost."

The tragedy of the cults manifests itself in many forms. Like the pain of a distraught woman whose daughter was marrying a Mormon. Like Julie, in the first part of this chap-

3. Brown, p. xx.

ter, the girl had been raised in a Christian home and sent to a Christian college where she fell in love with a returned Mormon missionary.

"Pastor Spencer," the woman told me, "my daughter says I can't even go to her wedding. Her fiance tells us that after the wedding, 'there will be no more discussion of religion.' We tried to talk to him but you won't believe what he told us."

"Try me."

"Well," she sniffed, "he said he knew how we felt. But we needed to remember that he was a returned missionary, and he was used to watching families cry as he led their children into Mormonism."

Three Basic Decisions

If we are going to meet the challenge of the cults, we must make some elementary decisions:

First, we must decide to defend ourselves against the cults. Many denominations will not mention the word Mormonism, much less take an open stand against it. None of the Christian television networks speaks openly about Mormonism. As an individual Christian, you must decide what your position is going to be.

Second, we must prepare for the battle. That means we must educate ourselves. Personally, it means you must read and study the cults and the biblical antidote. Corporately, the Church of Christ must preach and teach *openly* against cults. "Doctrine" can be a musty-sounding word. Julie, though she was the daughter of an evangelical minister, had no idea of the basic Christian theology of the Trinity. She was duck soup for such arguments as: "If there is only one God, to whom did Jesus pray in the Garden of Gethsemane?" We have to pay the price to educate ourselves and others.

Third, we must learn patience. One psychological study

on "snapping" (the phenomenon of extreme social alteration required to join a cult, see Appendix D) indicates that it may take years to jettison all the hang-ups of the cult. I find it takes as much as five years for an active Mormon to come out of the Mormon Church.

But no matter how long it takes we *must* pay the price of confrontation.

If we don't go, whom will God send?

Chapter Five

Opening the Dialogue

"In your book, you mentioned snapping. I think I have been experiencing that very thing, but I thought I was getting senile or losing my mind—I'm only 46!

"You said there were places in your mind that you couldn't go—what did that mean? I have found I am unable to think clearly and I have a hard time finding words that are normally in my vocabulary. I have been described by friends and relatives as possibly having had a minor stroke.

"I hope this doesn't last too long—but no matter, it is better this way than to be lost forever following the dictates of the Mormon Church."

Carol

Walk up to a Latter-day Saint and ask him, "Do you really believe in Mormonism?" He'll almost certainly answer, "Yes." I don't care if he hasn't been to church in ten years. Or if he's mad at all his Mormon friends and relatives. He's a "Mormon." We've all met Catholics who are "Catholic" even though they haven't been to church since their First Communion. That's what it is like to be a Mormon. A Presbyterian can become a Baptist without losing his family; a Methodist can join a Lutheran church without being ostracized from his society; but a Mormon *always* pays a price for leaving the Church. That means a Mormon professes to be Mormon regardless of doubts.

So you can see that your approach to your Mormon friend will depend upon how committed he is to the Church. Some people are unapproachable. Others are hungering for someone to talk to. The problem is discovering what level people are on.

The Mormon Commitment Level

Every Mormon exists somewhere between True Believer and Doubter. We can describe his level of commitment three ways: The True Believer, The Moderate Believer, and The Doubter.

Since we will approach different people differently, it will be necessary for us to evaluate the level of commitment. That will tell us where to begin.

Here is a brief breakdown of the three levels.

The hallmark of *The True Believer* is that he's an evangelist. He is convinced he has found the way of truth and he is ready to share it with others. He may be bold or shy, confident or self-conscious—those are personality traits. But whatever his nature, he is disposed, to the best of his ability, to declare his confidence in Mormonism.

The Moderate Believer, on the other hand, is more restrained in his faith. He's convinced in his own heart that Mormonism is the True Church, but he is tolerant of others. He understands that Mormonism is *his* religion. He believes it is true—perhaps "with every fiber of his being," as Mormons are fond of saying—but he holds out the possibility that he may be wrong. He will be less inclined than the True Believer to "bear you his testimony," though he probably would do so if you asked him.

The Doubter is no longer convinced that the Mormon Church is true. He continues to be a member, he may even go to church regularly, but he is no longer *sure.*

Now let's look at each of the three Mormon groups in more detail:

The True Believer

The True Believer can be either an Arrogant True Believer or a Naive True Believer.

The *Arrogant True Believer* is convinced that he's a member of the Only True Church, and he has never encountered serious challenge to his faith. That may be because he does not readily listen to *anything*. He may be brash. He is so convinced of his position that he pities those who are not Mormons.

At his worst, the Arrogant True Believer disdains non-Mormons as stupid if they don't immediately submit to Mormonism's gospel, and he's not above ridiculing those who disagree with him. If he's a boss he may resort to harassment of non-Mormon employees. Whether he is a convert or "born under the covenant," he has never seriously considered the possibility that Mormonism is wrong.

In his most deceived condition, the Arrogant True Believer has committed intellectual suicide. He is, as one friend describes it, "self-deceived." He has looked at reality and chosen to retreat into Mormonism. His conscience is seared. He may suffer from terminal spiritual deafness.

The *Naive True Believer* is also convinced about Mormonism. But, unlike his arrogant counterpart, the Naive True Believer is shocked to discover serious challenges to his faith.

I think I was a Naive True Believer. I can remember two incidents from my early Mormon experience that make me say that. First, on the very night I was baptized into the Mormon Church, I met a cheerful girl who was serving me in a cafeteria. She asked me why I was so happy and I told her I had just become a Mormon.

"Oh," she said, "I used to be a Mormon."

Her response shocked me. I couldn't believe that anyone ever left the Mormon Church. *Especially* not someone who appeared to be happy and cheerful. She should have been pining away in dejection if she had rejected the One True Church.

Another time I met the nicest middle-aged woman in an art class. In private conversation, I let slip that I was a new Mormon. She said the same thing the girl had said: "Oh, I used to be a Mormon."

For the rest of our acquaintance, I puzzled over how she could have left Mormonism without collapsing under the wrath of God. I'd have died for the Church. I was a Naive True Believer.

The Moderate Believer

The Moderate Believer is more subdued in his approach to his faith. He's tolerant. He respects other points of view.

The *Uninterested Moderate Believer* is not uninterested in Mormonism, he is uninterested in opposing opinions. The Uninterested Moderate Believer respects your right to believe what you want; therefore discussion is not particularly interesting to him.

The *Interested Moderate Believer,* on the other hand, wants to talk—if it can be done reasonably. He may simply have an academic interest in debate or he may be seeing things in Mormonism that disturb him. He may be on the verge of becoming a Doubter. He is a candidate for profitable discussion. If he really is objective, he'll respond to a realistic discussion of the problems of Mormonism.

But be careful with the Interested Moderate Believer, for he also presents one of our greatest opportunities to go wrong. He may not be what he seems! I often encounter Arrogant True Believers masquerading as Interested Moderate Believers.

These are people who only want to *appear* interested.

They are being deceptive. Their motives vary: perhaps it is
important to them to seem to be objective when they are not;
or they may be masquerading only in an attempt to convert
you to Mormonism; or, in the saddest cases, some of them
have no real interest in Mormonism at all—they are so confused that everything is simply a game to them.

The Doubter

The doubter has moved to objectivity. He has begun to see
something is wrong in Zion. He may only have a vague sense
of misgiving and may be quite defensive. With time, however, his doubts intensify. This does not mean he's ready to
leave Mormonism. He may be *years* from that—if, indeed,
he ever makes that choice. The Doubter has lots of options,
and if he is particularly afraid of or controlled by his family,
he may never seriously investigate his doubts. He may make
accommodations. In short, he may choose to live a lie.

The *Closet Doubter* is one who is not yet willing to discuss
his doubts openly. One of my teachers in college slipped into
a Baptist church during a showing of the movie "The God
Makers." Someone struck up a conversation after the film
and recognized that he had doubts, although he carefully attempted to conceal them. I was notified and telephoned him
at his home. He was very secretive, but we arranged a meeting. Those meetings have continued for two years. Today he
is open with me. He has concluded that the "Christ of Mormonism" is "too insipid to save." He's searching for God. As
yet, he remains a Closet Doubter.

The *Open Doubter* has dropped his pretensions. He is fed
up with defending the Mormon Church. He is nearly certain
it is false. Or at least so full of flaws as to be unredeemable.
He is looking for answers. He may find them in Christ, but
he may find them in another religious or social system.

Everyone is an individual. He has his own motives within
the confines of his private world. At best, we can only draw

him out into an objective discussion of truth as it exists in
Christ. To do so with cultists, we need to be aware of their
commitment to the organization. Only then can we determine how best to deal with them.

The best way to find out where Mormons are in this spec-
trum is to ask them. Asking questions opens doorways to
discovery. That's why every great salesman asks a lot of
questions. The answers allow people to reveal, indirectly
and without threat, where they are. To know what questions
to ask, we need to know whom we are talking to.

In the next chapter I will show you how to deal with each
of the three Mormon types.

Chapter Six

Encountering the Three Mormon Types

"Thank God I chose to read your book! After seven active and dedicated years in the Mormon Church, I had found myself depressed, confused, and with many doubts and questions. [And I discovered] how little the leaders answer your questions.... I feel cheated, deceived, and spiritually raped by a doctrine and philosophy that I embraced and trusted. It has been more than difficult to break away from the hold that Joseph Smith and his Book of Mormon have on me....

"It's hard to believe that those seemingly sincere and gentle men could continue to perpetuate such a lie. It's also hard to believe that those I have come to dearly love may remain blindly devoted to this deception, for I believe that what I have discovered will have little impact on them...."

Kathryn

Each of the three distinct Mormon types requires a different approach. I sincerely believe each type can be reached. We bear the responsibility of approaching each with as much love, vigor, and accuracy as we can muster.

On the other hand, we must remember that ultimately

only the individual himself can make the final decision. Every man will be responsible for his own soul at the judgment. In any missionary encounter three persons are involved: the witnessee, the witnesser, and God. You are only responsible for your individual role. If it is biblical, then you have done all you can do. As my friend Charles Trombly, a former Jehovah's Witness, says, "We are in sales; God is in management. Don't try to do His job." Paul said it this way: "One waters, another plants, but God gives the increase."

We can be sure, when we obey God's injunction to "go into all the world and make disciples," that He will attend us with gifts of grace to make it possible for those we encounter to hear and respond. Therefore, we do our best in the most godly way we can, and then we leave the results in the hands of God.

The Discussion with the True Believer

The True Believer, in one way, is the easiest of all with whom to deal because he is the least likely to listen!

My advice in dealing with True Believers is to keep your expectations low, and to witness with great boldness.

Keeping your expectations low means to follow sales manager Robert Ringer's unexpected injunction to "maintain a positive attitude by *anticipating* a negative outcome." When you understand that most sales calls do not result in sales, you will be more likely to risk witnessing. Witnessing really is salesmanship—presenting the good news in a package that can be heard, understood, and believed. But most missionary encounters do not result in converts. That's a fact. Jesus said, "Straight is the gate, and narrow the way that leads to eternal life and few there be who find it." Paul said, "Through the foolishness of preaching, *some* are saved." That means that whenever you encounter True Believers you must understand that there is *little* chance they are about to change. They are the most firmly entrenched in Mormonism.

By deciding to be obedient, whether or not you get to see results, you will be emboldened. This can be a great evangelistic tool. Let me illustrate:

Mary is not a Mormon, but I am going to include her story because it illustrates boldness as a tool for dealing with *any* cult. Mary is a missionary for the Unification Church. She first contacted me at my office, representing herself as a "Christian worker." I quickly sensed her affiliation and asked her point blank, "Are you a member of the Unification Church?"

"Yes, I am," she replied. "But I don't want to talk to you about that. I want to talk to you about some political concerns. . . ."

"Well," I said, "that would be wasting your time and mine. I am very familiar with the Unification Church and with the front organizations like CAUSA—and I'm not interested."

"Just like that?"

"Just like that."

"May I ask why?"

'You may, but I'm not sure you want to. Look, here's the nub of the problem. You and I are on different teams. I think you are in emotional and psychological bondage to a spirit of Antichrist. And it is going to do us no good to discuss anything."

Mary was taken aback. "How can you say those things?"

"My dear, I say those things after much study and prayer. Your leaders are false prophets who keep thousands brainwashed while humiliating them by sending them out to sell flowers."

In her missionary endeavors, Mary had probably never been spoken to so directly.

"You sound very sure of yourself," she said.

"I *am* very sure of myself. Here is my message for you.

'It's not too late. Repent! Flee the wrath to come. Flee the judgment of God.' "

She stared blankly at me.

"Listen," I said softly. "I told you that you probably wouldn't want to know what I think."

She looked steadily at me and said, "But I do want to know what you think, because I have some doubts about my faith."

I'll admit, I didn't believe her. But my witnessing philosophy had allowed me to challenge her and now that same philosophy forced me to follow up.

It was worth five minutes to find out.

Those five minutes turned into two hours.

Two weeks later she came back and watched a video on the Moonies.

Two months later she came back, brought me some pumpkin bread, and spent another two hours listening to me explain the Gospel of Christ. I gave her some books and we talked about the saving blood of Christ and the infallibility of His Word.

As I write this, Mary and I have had a dozen meetings. Once while she was on vacation she wrote me saying, "Sometimes, Jim, I don't think I can stay in the Unification Church another day." I have prayed with her that Jesus would come into her life. She has prayed, "*If* the Unification Church is wrong, then I renounce it." I don't know that she'll ever leave the Moonies; she may not. But my point is that no one had ever talked to Mary the way I did. It shocked her, but it also touched some deeply rooted doubts within her. For a moment the mask was ripped aside and she took a risk: She risked trusting me with her doubts. When she found out I wouldn't violate her, she opened up even further.

The point is that when you encounter True Believers, you may as well risk a bold shot. You really have nothing to lose. This is a tactic some Mormon experts call "knocking the polish off their testimony."

Here's one more example of an encounter with a True Believer.

Bob, the manager of a local restaurant, struck up a casual acquaintance with me. He learned that I was a former Mormon and asked me about it.

"Yes," I said. "I was a Mormon Elder for ten years."

Bob, a Mormon, got an incredibly pained look on his face. "Why? How could you leave The Truth?"

Bob appeared to me to be a True Believer, and I suspected that he was an Arrogant True Believer. So I answered, "I didn't leave The Truth. I left error."

Before he could interrupt, I continued, "Bob, I had no option when I learned the facts about Mormonism. I *had* to leave."

"What facts?"

"The fact that Joseph Smith was a false prophet, that the Book of Mormon is not true."

"Well, that is your opinion." I knew Bob must be thinking of the classic True Believer position that the Book of Mormon was *singularly without the error of other books.*

"No, it isn't my *opinion*," I said. "It is hard fact. See, Joseph said he translated the Book of Mormon from gold plates by 'the gift and power of God.' That it was the most perfect of any book on the face of the earth. But, in reality, the Book of Mormon has been changed nearly four thousand times in the last hundred and fifty years."

"That's not true!"

"Let me ask you a question. Do you really believe the Book of Mormon has not been changed?"

"Of course it hasn't been changed. That is just a lot of nonsense thought up by enemies of the Church."

And now I slowed 'way down in my speech, checked my breathing, and launched into the first of my three objectives in witnessing to a Mormon.

Rule Number One: Isolate. In dealing with all cultists it is important to nail down—isolate—the subject of discussion.

If you do not, you are set for a long series of meaningless trips around spiritual mulberry bushes. I isolated our subject with Bob by asking him to deal with one very specific subject: Had changes been made in the Book of Mormon?

"Okay. Let me define some terms. If the 1830 Book of Mormon was different from the one you are reading, would you admit changes had occurred?"

"There haven't been any."

"What would the implications be if there were?"

"What do you mean?"

"Well, if Joseph Smith says God gave him a perfect book and if later it was changed, wouldn't you admit that Joseph was wrong?"

"It hasn't been changed."

"But *if* it *had* been."

"But it hasn't."

This tedious process of nailing down the premise is very important. I may only have one shot with this guy. If I don't clarify exactly what I am talking about, he will slip out of the conversation without being challenged. I must get him nailed down to one *point*. One very specific point.

Now I turn to my next objective.

Rule Number Two: Qualify. By this I mean ask the Mormon to qualify or change his position, if you are proved to be right. With Bob I said, "*If* the Book of Mormon has been changed in important ways, would you admit that it is not what Joseph Smith said it was?"

"I've already told you—"

"Bob, I understand you don't think it's been changed. If it hasn't, you're right and I'm wrong. But, just for the sake of discussion, answer my question."

"Okay," he sighed. "For the sake of argument, if the Book of Mormon has been changed, then it isn't what Joseph Smith said it was. But, I testify to you that it hasn't been changed."

"I know you believe that," I said. "I once believed that, but

I don't anymore. But what either of us believes is not important. What is important is what the truth is, wouldn't you
agree?"

"Of course."

"Wouldn't you also agree that if we had an 1830 Book of
Mormon here, as well as a recent one, that we could answer
this question very quickly?"

"Sure." Bob must have felt safe for two reasons; first, he
was absolutely convinced the Book of Mormon was true;
second, he could see I didn't have an 1830 Book of Mormon.

"Well, obviously, I don't have an 1830 Book of Mormon
with me, but they are available. As a matter of fact, the
Mormon Church makes photocopies of them readily available."

Now it was Bob's turn to interrupt. "Well, that ought to
prove that it *hasn't* been changed. If it had, why would the
Church make it easily available?"[1]

"The Church, in 1980, issued a photo-reprint of the 1830
Book of Mormon. It was printed on the same kind of paper
as the 1830 book, the same size and shape. It was issued as
memorabilia for the hundred-and-fiftieth anniversary of the
organization of the Mormon Church. Deseret Book Company printed it with the blessings of the First Presidency. It
was sold in Mormon bookstores for twenty-five dollars."

"Is it still on sale?"

"Yes, although sometimes it is kept under the counter and
you have to press the salesperson to get it. It seems that Latter-day Saints were not particularly interested in purchasing
it. Some realize that most people who buy it are using it to
prove that changes have been made. I have purchased a
dozen or more copies.

1. I chose not to ask Bob to deal with the implication of his statement:
    Somewhere within him, he obviously thought the Church would
    suppress, or at least not make readily available, evidence that put it
    in a bad light. Rather, I stuck to the one *specific point*—that the Book
    of Mormon has been changed.

"But, Bob," I continued, "the point is that anyone who wants to find out if I'm lying can do so by buying an 1830 reprint. So, you can tell me that it isn't true. You can tell me that you have a testimony that the Book of Mormon was translated by the gift and power of God. But the fact is that anyone who wants to find out if the Book of Mormon is true can do so. You don't have to rely on your subjective experience.

"See, Bob, either I am lying or the Church is. Every Mormon prophet has reiterated the Church's formal position, that 'the Book of Mormon is the most perfect book on the face of the earth, translated by the gift and power of God, singularly without the errors of other books.' In fact, Joseph Fielding Smith, when he was President of the Church, was asked if it was true that changes had been made. He said, 'Only sons of Belial would say that there have been thousands of changes in the Book of Mormon.'[2]

"Well, Bob, somebody is either wrong or lying. Now the ball is in your court. I am telling you that *anybody* who wants to know the truth can find out for himself. . . ."

I stuck to the point with Bob. He finally agreed to look for himself and I was now at the third of my three objectives in witnessing to a Mormon. I must verify.

Rule Number Three: Verify. By this I mean that when you have isolated a point to discuss with your Mormon friend, and when you have gotten him to agree to qualify his position if you are proved correct, then it is time to verify your point. With Bob I completed the third rule by sending him information in the mail verifying our subject of discussion.

Bob and I have now had several conversations. He always wants to go around the mulberry bush, but I make him stick to one specific point. It is a point I choose—a point I am very sure of. A point that I can document thoroughly. Only time will tell how Bob will ultimately respond. With True Believ-

2.   *The Improvement Era,* December 1961, pp. 924-925.

ers, the only course you can follow is to "knock the polish off their testimony" by coming on strong and gentle, tough and tender, bold and specific.

Encountering Moderate Believers

Moderate Believers need to be handled a little more gently. They are more likely to talk reasonably with you. They'll hear you out. But they may not be interested in pursuing the conversation very far—especially if they are Uninterested Moderate Believers. Therefore, we want to treat them with deference and respect. Nevertheless, we need to be firm and purposeful. Our goal is still to get them to *specific points* that can be argued with objective evidence.

When I feel I am encountering a Moderate Believer, I use diagnostic questions to find out if he is Interested or Uninterested. In the case I'm about to describe, I used a different point than I used with Bob.

It is often good to focus on the Book of Mormon, however, because all Mormons realize that the Book of Mormon story is central to the credibility of Mormonism. Also, it is easy to demonstrate, objectively, that the Book of Mormon has been changed thousands of times.

Be sure to keep our three objectives in mind: Isolate, Qualify, Verify.

To repeat for emphasis:

The first step is to isolate the subject of discussion—in this case, the subject is the validity of the Book of Mormon.

Then, you must qualify your prospect. You do this by getting a commitment from your contact that *if you prove your point,* he will make some change in his thinking. In other words, *if* you demonstrate that the Book of Mormon has been changed, your friend must admit that it will make a difference to him. *You have to get that commitment before you prove your point.* Nothing is more disconcerting than going to the trouble to document and prove a point only to have your contact shrug his shoulders and move on to another subject.

Once you have isolated and qualified your prospect, you then need only verify—provide irrefutable documentation—to win your point, and hopefully move your friend down the commitment scale toward Doubter.

Here is how I used qualifying questions to approach one Moderate Believer—my mother-in-law.

Audrey, was raised in England. She met my father-in-law there during the war. Audrey was unfamiliar with Mormonism before she met him, but after she married him and moved to a tiny Mormon settlement in Idaho, she discovered that religion was going to be a very important part of her life. Eventually she converted and became a fully active and believing Mormon. However, she has never had the same stubborn determination of her husband.

On several occasions she opened up to my wife, Margaretta, sharing some of her deeper, rather un-Mormon thoughts. She was a Moderate Believer, keeping her heretical thoughts pretty much to herself.

One Monday, Audrey called my home and said she wanted to see the movie "The God Makers," which we show every Tuesday night at our church. Margaretta and I were shocked. Audrey showed up, watched the movie, then said to me, "Well, that's not so bad." She was very gracious and good-natured. "I don't agree with everything," she said, "but there is some truth in it."

"But it doesn't disturb you?"

"No, not really. Oh, some parts of it are way off-base. . . ."

I was quite surprised by her reaction. Pressing on I said, "Well, we are going to show the next movie, 'The Temple of the God Makers.' Would you like to watch it?"

"Sure."

Now, "The Temple of the God Makers" introduces little that is not covered in "The God Makers," so I was really caught off-guard by her reaction to it—she was steaming mad! What upset her was an animated sequence that shows the Mormon god, Elohim, walking up to the door of the Virgin Mary to conceive Jesus.

Audrey was furious. "That is a cheap shot. That is not what we believe at all."

"What do you mean?" I asked.

"We do not believe that Mary had sexual relations with God the Father. We believe she conceived by the Holy Ghost."

"Well," I said slowly, "I'm glad you believe that. That is the orthodox belief. But it isn't what Mormonism teaches."

"It certainly is! Mary was overshadowed by the Holy Ghost."

I could see she was prepared to stick to her guns. On the other hand, it was obvious she did not know Mormon doctrine on this point.

So, my next step was to *qualify* her position. But what should the qualifying statement be? Obviously, it is a little early to say something like "*If* I can prove to you that the Mormon Church teaches that the god Elohim had sexual relations with Mary, *then* will you leave the Church?" That is too radical.

Audrey is obviously—and rightly—disgusted at the concept of natural relations as the mode of Christ's conception. I want to ask her a qualifying question that will demonstrate that her beliefs are not what Mormonism teaches. In other words, I want her to begin to question the authority of the Mormon Church in her life.

So I settle for a small gain. I ask this question: "Audrey, we could argue all night about whether or not the Mormon Church teaches natural relations between Elohim and Mary. You say the Church does not teach that and I say it does. But, let me ask you, *if I could show you statements from five General Authorities of the Church, saying that Elohim had natural relations with Mary, would you agree that the Church teaches that?"*

Now we went through the but-it-doesn't; yes-it-does routine for a few minutes. Finally she agreed that if I could give her the five statements she would agree that the Church taught it.

Then I provided the documentation. (See Chapter Twelve.)

Quite a small gain, right?

I agree, but small gains add up. After I sent the verifying documentation, I unexpectedly dropped by my in-laws' home. My material was spread out on the table, along with all sorts of Mormon Church books. Both Audrey and my father-in-law were actively studying the subject that had so upset Audrey. And they were sure to find that I was right.

Now, other doors have begun to open with Margaretta's parents. They receive my monthly newsletter, "Through the Maze." And they have come to our church a couple of times. Recently, Audrey asked Margaretta to do a musical program for her Stake Relief Society Banquet. Margaretta sang and shared—in her old home ward—with one hundred lovely Mormon ladies.

The subject of Mormonism comes up regularly now between us and our in-laws. The tension is nearly gone. And I believe Audrey has been downgraded from a Moderate Believer to at least a Closet Doubter.

Encountering Doubters

Doubters are the easiest to encounter. Simply ask them a huge qualifying question like, "If I could prove to you that thousands of changes have been made in the Book of Mormon, would you leave the Mormon Church?"

The reason for asking the qualifying questions is to see how ready the person is for change. There is no sense proving to a Doubter that Joseph Smith is a false prophet unless the contact is going to do something about it.

You say that *nobody* could remain a Mormon and believe that Joseph Smith was a false prophet. Well, thousands of people go to the Mormon Church every Sunday knowing that.

I have a friend who knows Joseph Smith was a false prophet. And he knows that the Book of Mormon is not Scripture. And yet he is a Mormon college professor! None of his friends knows about his doubts. He is in church several times a week, holds responsible positions in the Church, and holds a temple recommend. And he is one of thousands. He says someday he will have the courage to leave. But right now his concerns for his family, his job, and his friends keep him from being honest.

Encountering the three Mormon types becomes easy with practice. As you learn to relax and *let God do the managing,* you are released to make sales calls. And occasionally, just like in selling or fishing, you land a big one.

Chapter Seven

Expanding the Encounter

"I read your book ... three times in two days. My husband was furious. He told me to get that 'anti' book out of our house. He said if I left the Church, he'd leave me. I was crushed ... I don't want to lose my husband. ... If I'm excommunicated from the Church, my father-in-law will be one of the brethren present at the court to judge me.

"I would like to ... talk to a pastor about these things, but my brother-in-law made it quite clear that if I do I will be excommunicated. ...

"For some reason through all of this, I can't shake the feeling that God cares. ..."

Robin

When I was in the Navy we were on patrol in the South China Sea during what was then known as the "Laotian Crisis" (which would escalate into the Vietnam War). One afternoon we were called to General Quarters; a two-man reconnaissance jet had gone down and we were being sent out to rescue the crew.

We did save the co-pilot, who told us this grisly story.

It seems the pilot of the jet was one of the best in his squadron. He could fly in and out of places under the noses of enemy radar without being shot down. But this time the plane had been hit and the men had to ditch it.

The pilot, in his determination to fly better than anyone else, had earlier rigged his seat belts in a special way so that he could better take the G-forces of his aircraft. When the two men bailed out, the explosive charges that blew their seats out of the plane worked fine. They were blasted clear of the craft. The co-pilot released his seat belt and his seat fell away into the ocean as he parachuted slowly down. But he watched with horror as his pilot struggled to release his modified seat belt mechanism. He watched helplessly as the pilot, unable to get free from the heavy seat, plunged into the sea and sank.

I thought of that experience one evening years later, after I had been born again and was reading the book of Romans. Paul is writing to the Church of Christ in Rome about his brothers, the Jews. What he said is what I feel about my Mormon people:

> My brothers, how I wish with all my heart that my own people might be saved! How I pray to God for them! I can assure you that they are deeply devoted to God; but their devotion is not based on true knowledge. They have not known the way in which God puts people right with himself, and instead, they have tried to set up their own way; and so they did not submit themselves to God's way of putting people right. For Christ has brought the Law to an end, so that everyone who believes is put right with God (Romans 10:1–4, Good News Bible).

The mistake the Jews made was to re-rig the seat belt. God had provided for their safety through the Law but they'd tinkered with, expanded, explained, re-rigged their own protection. They so badly wanted to do the right thing that they did the wrong thing.

And that is the mistake the Mormons have made. Wanting to do right is not the same as doing right.

I remember reading a newspaper article telling of a young

babysitter who put the baby in the bathtub and then plugged in a radio and set it on the edge of the tub. The babysitter wanted to entertain the baby during the bath. She wanted to do right. Her intentions were good. But the radio fell into the bath water; the baby was electrocuted.

The babysitter's actions were not dishonorable—they simply were wrong. God has provided the sacrifice of Christ, and our faith in that sacrifice, as the payment for sin. Mormonism and other cults that rewrite the rules may be very well-intentioned, but they are wrong. "There is a way," the Bible says, "that seems right to a man, but in the end it leads to death" (Proverbs 14:12).

The Ministry of Reconciliation

Growing up in a little town in the badlands of Wyoming, I used to hear our town whistle blow six times a day so everybody knew what time it was. When the noon whistle blew all the dogs in town would start howling and the townspeople would check their watches to see if they were correct. If not, they changed them, "reconciled" them to the standard set at the center of town.

The Bible says we Christians are called to the task of "reconciling men to God in Christ" (see 2 Corinthians 5:18). Reconciling men with God means causing them to make adjustments so they are no longer out of kilter with God. Men are born out of step with God because, in the Garden of Eden, our ancestors chose to move in disobedience to God. The harmony Adam and Eve had with God was destroyed.

Dr. Robert Gange, a research scientist who has been cited seven times by NASA for "creative development of technology," says there is evidence that the Fall in the Garden may well have disturbed the genetic code. He suggests that the misery of human nature (our inability to live in peace, our terrible psychological problems, our propensity to sin) may be tied up in our very physical nature—as a direct result of the Fall.

Our job, as disciples, is to bring people to Christ in order to restore the right relationship between man and God. Sometimes, as in Mormonism, it's necessary to shake people loose from false theology, to make them aware that the system in which they are trusting is unable to save them.

When we deal with cultists, sometimes the Word of God has to destroy before it can rebuild. When God sent Jeremiah to the Israelites, he was sent to "uproot and tear down, to destroy and overthrow, to build and to plant" (Jeremiah 1:10).

As we destroy the false religious system of the cultist we also have to present the Gospel to him. We chop out a piece of false doctrine and we replace it with the truth. It is like rebuilding a highway: The new construction rips out the old highway a little at a time, replacing it with new. Eventually the old road is taken out of commission entirely.

Spiritual Warfare of the Highest Order

It is well to remember that unless God does a supernatural work, no one can be saved (see Matthew 19:25–26). Before being born again, people are spiritually dead (see Ephesians 2:1) and blinded by Satan (see 2 Corinthians 4:4).

Therefore, it is absolutely necessary that as you witness you pray for the Holy Spirit to lead you to the words that will penetrate the veil of blindness, words that will make their way into the cultist's mind.

We minister intellectually, with words. We put information into the conscious mind of the hearer. We preach sound doctrine to him and combat philosophical and spiritual error. But there is another dimension that is beyond our pale—the spiritual dimension. Our only weapon there is prayer. So, for me, it is useful to visualize the hearer's "inner man" as divided into conscious and subconscious or spirit and soul. We reach the conscious or soulish level. God reaches the unconscious or spiritual realm. (See Chart A: "Cooperating with God in Soul-Winning" on page 74.)

Reversing the Process

The *process* of coming into Mormonism is a reasoning process. The Mormon missionary takes you down a railroad track—his carefully prepared railroad track. He takes you into areas of discussion that are new to you. He asks esoteric questions you have never considered. He is confident and well-prepared. Your objections are, necessarily, ill-prepared, because you have not had time to think through and discover the flaws in his reasoning.

I experienced this process myself. I was bright enough but I was not a Christian. And I was needy—I needed stability in my life. The Mormon message of assurance and stability and clean living was appealing to me. I needed to come out of sin. I was sick and tired of my lifestyle. What I needed was Christ, but what I got was a loving group who thought they had truth, but who in reality had emptiness and deception.

These were dear people who had been programmed with faulty information. They were innocently in error. And they, in turn, programmed me with the same error.

The Bible talks about "sophisticated reasoning," "worldly philosophy that can take us captive," and warfare against "spiritual wickedness in high places."

The only solution, the Bible says, to this kind of error is to "demolish strongholds ... arguments and every pretension that sets itself up against the [accurate] knowledge of God, [to] take captive every *thought* to make it obedient to Christ" (2 Corinthians 10:4-5). The Greek in that passage tells us that the "thoughts" the apostle Paul is talking about are "designs"—carefully constructed arguments with our spiritual destruction as their end.

*Mormons are won to Mormonism by carefully constructed
arguments; they will be won out of Mormonism as we take
the arguments apart, brick by brick.* They will come out the
same door they went in.

The question is, who will respond to the cults? Mormon
missionaries give two years of their lives to preach a gospel
they innocently believe to be God's plan of salvation but
which, in reality, was forged in the fiery councils of hell to
lead men to eternal damnation.

Who will educate themselves to combat the cults?

Whom can God send?

Who will sit down with Latter-day Saints and take apart
the sophistication of the devil, line upon line?

If you are to be one of those, then the next sections of this
book will be a crash course to educate you to encounter
Mormonism—and to win the encounter.

CHART A
COOPERATING WITH GOD IN SOUL-WINNING

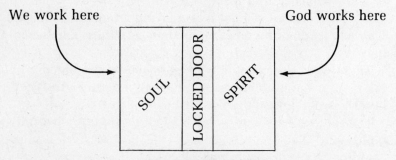

THE INNER MAN

We input witnessing information in the form of Scripture,
testimony, and reason. Sometimes the process seems to be
going nowhere.

But the energy of the witness, *coupled with* prayer, coop-
erates with the Spirit of God to produce a climate in which
the hearer *may* choose life. A climate in which the door to
salvation can be opened.

Part 2

Encounters of The Best Kind

Chapter Eight

The Nature of God

"On the subject of divorce the bishop was very bluntly clear and his tone was stern! He explained that since I had, by accepting the Good News, blocked my wife's 'eternal progression' . . . she did have the right to seek a divorce and find a mate that could satisfy her desire for a Celestial Marriage. I asked the bishop if he could find scriptural support for this point of view and he said, 'I don't know of any.' "

David

BYU professor James E. Ford sums up Mormon theology this way:

> Mormon doctrine means that ultimately we are not dependent upon God for our existence. And since we can make ourselves as godly as the Father, we don't feel any jealousy toward him.[1]

Joseph Smith claimed: "Man is co-equal with God himself."[2] God, Joseph said, found himself among spirits and glory.[3]

Cults always part company with the Church of Christ over the nature of God. And with Mormonism, the doctrinal

1. *Newsweek*, "What Mormons Believe," September 1, 1980, p. 68.
2. *History of the Church*, Vol. 6, pp. 310-312.
3. Joseph Fielding Smith, *Teachings of the Prophet Joseph Smith*, Deseret Book Company, Salt Lake City, 1977, p. 354.

differences are fundamental and irreconcilable. It is essential and extremely profitable to discuss this subject with Latter-day Saints. The discussion of the nature of God is, as far as I'm concerned, the best dialogue we can have with Mormons.

You must prepare yourself, however, to talk accurately about the nature of God. You don't have to be a theologian, but you do need a working understanding of His nature. You need to be sure of your own theology in order to understand the basic doctrinal errors that continue to crop up in the cults.

So these pages are designed to help us review our own beliefs as a foundation for discussions with a Latter-day Saint.

Monotheism: The Correct Choice.

To understand the error of Mormon theology, it is helpful to look at the choices one faces when thinking about God. (See Chart B: "Thinking About God" on pages 80–81.)

The first choice a man makes is between theism and atheism. Theism is the term for someone who believes in God; an atheist does *not* believe in God.

Atheists do not believe in a Creator God. They are materialists. They believe that all we see in nature is the result of matter, which was not created, but which has eternally existed. Materialists believe that the universe had no beginning. That, throughout time, it simply pulsates from one Big Bang to another, evolving only through natural law.

Theists, on the other hand, believe in some kind of Creator. But, they may be deists, pantheists, dualists, polytheists, or monotheists.

A *deist* believes in one Creator God. But the God of the deist has withdrawn from His universe. He is the clockmaker who wound up the universe and now leaves it to run according to natural law. He doesn't interfere in any miraculous or supernatural way.

A *pantheist* is one who believes that the universe *is* God. In other words, the sum total of all creation adds up to God.

A *dualist* believes in a Good God and an Evil God who are locked in mortal combat for the universe. There are few dualists around these days. Zoroastrianism was one of the grander expressions of dualism.

A *polytheist* believes in many gods. Polytheism is the formula of Hinduism, which boasts millions of gods.

Only *monotheists* believe in the God of the Bible. *A monotheist believes in one Creator God who is separate from His universe, but present in it and actively involved with it.* There are only three monotheistic groups: Jews, Muslims, and Christians. All three of these groups trace their history back to Abraham. Jews and Muslims fail to recognize Jesus Christ as God incarnate in human flesh.

Degeneration to Polytheism

Polytheism is the belief in the existence of more than one God. (Note: it is not essential to *worship* more than one god to be a polytheist—it is merely necessary to believe in their existence. *Poly*-many, *theos*-god.)

Polytheism fails to answer the philosophical questions of creation. Polytheism fails to *ask* these questions: "Where did the god I am worshiping come from? How was he created? If he is not the First Cause, who is?"

Polytheists, by failing to ask these questions, end up blindly serving demi-gods.

Polytheism is paganism. It is a degeneration of thought. In the past, anthropologists taught that monotheism evolved *upwards out of* polytheism. The scenario was that primitive man saw lightning fall and worshiped the god of lightning. He saw fire and worshiped the fire god. Eventually he evolved to the worship of the gods of Greek and Roman mythology. And, finally, as he became more sophisticated, he decided to believe in one God.

CHART B
THINKING ABOUT GOD

The fundamental theological error of Mormonism is polytheism. I have found the following diagrams helpful in talking to Mormons about the nature of God. I have drawn this chart on napkins in restaurants and on blank Bible pages. I like to follow it with a study of monotheism from Isaiah 43–46.

Everyone must either be a theist or an atheist.

If he is a theist, he believes in some kind of Supreme Being.

If he is a theist, he still has choices to make.

He may be a *polytheist*: one who believes in the existence of many gods. Mormonism teaches that all worthy Mormons may become gods.

Or he may be a *pantheist*: one who believes that God is the sum-total of His universe, and indistinguishable from it.

He may be a *deist*: one who believes in a creator who made the universe, and then departed from it to leave it to run by itself.

He may be a *dualist*: one who believes in both a good god and an evil god.

Finally, a person may be a *monotheist*: one who believes in a personal Creator God who is throughout His universe but distinct from it. He is omnipresent: everywhere present *in* His universe, but He is *not* the universe.

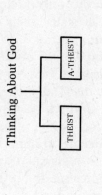

Thinking About God

THEIST — A-THEIST

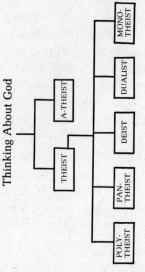

Thinking About God

THEIST — A-THEIST

POLY-THEIST | PAN-THEIST | DEIST | DUALIST | MONO-THEIST

Thinking About God

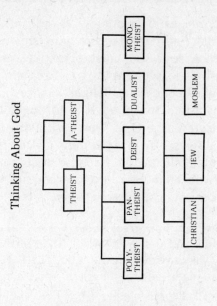

The God of monotheism is the God of biblical revelation.

No one "evolves" into monotheism from polytheism. History (particularly the history of the Bible) demonstrates that the reverse is true: God reveals Himself to His people, but they lose their knowledge of Him and follow "other" gods. The Bible is the story of God calling men to worship Him as He really is—the One True and Living God. All Judeo-Christian thought centers around the fact that in all the universe there is but one God.

Mormonism disqualifies itself as a Christian religion by its stubborn determination to declare that many gods exists. And that men evolve to become gods *themselves.*

However, recent anthropological research indicates that
monotheism actually predates polytheism. The *Encyclopaedia Britannica* says the most primitive societies actually
were monotheistic, worshiping one Creator God. This is the
anthropological concept of "High God."[4]

Christians teach that God has, throughout the ages, revealed Himself as the One True and Living God, beginning
with His fellowship with Adam and Eve in the Garden.

But the Bible tells us that because of sin mankind became
separated from God, lost intimate contact with Him, and
eventually became completely degenerate:

> The Lord saw how great man's wickedness on the earth
> had become, and that every inclination of the thoughts of
> his heart was only evil all the time. The Lord was grieved
> that he had made man on the earth, and his heart was filled
> with pain. So the Lord said, "I will wipe mankind, whom I
> have created, from the face of the earth . . ." (Genesis 6:5-7).

After the Flood, God restored fellowship with mankind.
But again man degenerated into wickedness and occult worship. It was out of evil, polytheistic Babylon that God called
Abraham to the Promised Land where He sought to establish a people to worship Him and to avoid the polytheistic
worship of Egypt and Babylonia.

The heartbeat of the Old Testament is the story of God
calling His people away from the worship of "stumps and
stones"—that is, the worship of idols made out of wood and
stone. God censured Israelites because they had "prostituted
themselves to other gods" (Judges 2:17). But the Israelites
continued to intermarry with pagans and to worship the
Baals and Asharah poles. Even Solomon returned to honoring the polytheistic gods of the pagans.

God, in every age, has commanded men to worship Him

4. *Encyclopaedia Britannica*, 1981, Vol. v, pp. 35-36, Vol. 14, p. 1042.

and Him alone. But, because of man's degenerate nature, he has sought power from the dark world of the occult. And the evil one, the enemy of our souls, is always ready to respond through demon powers.

Joseph Smith entered the religious arena through the door of the occult. (See Chapter Three.) He did not have well-defined ideas about God, and he abandoned the Bible for necromancy, communication with spirits of the dead supposedly to learn future events. As time went on he developed his ideas about God into a polytheistic nightmare.

The Polytheism of Mormonism

When Joseph Smith said, "God found himself among spirits," he showed his paganism, because God by definition must predate everything else. He is the Creator, the Prime Mover, the First Cause. Anything greater, bigger, older, more knowledgeable or more powerful than God, would *itself* be God! Any being who "finds himself" in the midst of other gods must, himself, have had a creator.

Nothing can predate God. He is first, or as He says, "I am the Alpha and the Omega," the first and the last (Revelation 1:8).

But Joseph Smith not only believed and taught polytheism, *he boasted about it!* He claimed he had "always preached plurality of Gods," and told his congregation:

> You have got to learn how to be Gods yourselves ... the same as all Gods have done before you ... until you are able to dwell in everlasting burnings and to sit in glory.[5]

Brigham Young, as he so often did, expanded Joseph's thinking, saying, "Man is King of Kings and Lord of Lords in embryo."[6]

5. *Journal of Discourses*, Vol. 6, p. 4.
6. *Journal of Discourses*, Vol. 10, p. 223.

Eventually, Mormon apostle Orson Pratt would say that there were more gods than there are particles of matter in a million planets like the earth.[7]

Today, every active Mormon is a polytheist, although he probably would not use that term. Every active, orthodox Latter-day Saint recites: "As man is, God once was; and as God is, man may become." *Every practicing Mormon hopes that one day he himself will be a god.*

In addition to believing that men can become gods, Mormonism teaches an infinite number of gods. Orson Pratt stated:

> We were begotten by our Father in Heaven; the person of our Father in Heaven was begotten on a previous heavenly world by His Father; and again, He was begotten by a still more ancient Father and so on, from generation to generation, from one heavenly world to another still more ancient, until our minds are wearied and lost in the multiplicity of generations and successive worlds, and as a last resort, we wonder in our mind, how far back the genealogy extends, and how the first world was formed, and how the first Father was begotten.[8]

Those are exactly the right questions Mormons should, but fail to, ask. Pratt tells us we shouldn't bother thinking about the first Father—that it is a waste of time. Such speculation, he says, would simply produce an endless succession of personal gods. Let's not trouble ourselves with the question because *"in worshipping any one of these Gods, we worship the whole."*[9]

Thus, Mormonism starts in midstream, worshiping a god who happens to be "our" god, since he's in charge of this world.

---

7. *Journal of Discourses,* Vol. 2, p. 345.
8. Orson Pratt, *The Seer,* Washington, D.C., 1854, p. 132.
9. Pratt, p. 132.

Most Latter-day Saints have not really thought through the implications of their polytheism. They have a vague sense that there are lots of worlds and lots of gods, and they believe they are destined for godhood. As strange as it seems, concerning beginnings, Mormons are required to believe two *different* theories at the same time. First, they believe they are co-eternal with the rest of the gods. On the other hand, they believe they were born spiritually to the God Elohim and existed as "spirit children" in heaven before they came to earth to "take on a body" (natural birth).

Mormons commonly think of God as "Heavenly Father" (Elohim). Jesus is one of Elohim's spirit sons, "the Savior." Satan was another and, for that matter, so were all the men of the earth, as well as all the demons. Thus, Elohim is your spirit father, the spirit father of Jesus, and also the spirit father of Satan. Which makes you, Jesus, and Satan brothers.

The process by which God has spirits is a little foggy, although most Mormon theologians teach that Elohim has several spirit wives by whom he conceives his spirit offspring. He experienced mortality on another planet, where he received a body and eventually, through the process called "eternal progression," has come to be our God.[10]

That means that throughout the universe men are becoming gods, receiving dominion over their own planets and conceiving spirit children in heaven so they can send them to earth to be born in mortality and repeat the process, "worlds without end."

Such theology is philosophically and emotionally unsatisfying and it can be difficult to discuss. But there is a way to talk to Latter-day Saints about the nature of God. A way which can lead to a real breakthrough.

10.   McConkie, pp. 238–239; *Journal of Discourses*, Vol. 6, p. 3.

How to Talk to Mormons About the Nature of God

To talk to Mormons about the nature of God, you need to do these things:

First, you need to commit them to the fact of their polytheism.

Second, you need to demonstrate the philosophical basis for monotheism. That is, to walk them through to the logical conclusion that God *cannot* have been created.

Third, then you can show them that the Bible is clearly and absolutely monotheistic.

That may sound like a rather large order, but it's a process you can learn—and fairly simply. I really suggest you study this chapter through several times and then go through these three points in order.

First, commit them to polytheism. Your Latter-day Saint friends will be reluctant to admit to polytheism. In fact, many of them will not even be familiar with the term. You will need to clarify terms. The phrase they *do* understand is "plurality of gods."

Be patient and stick to the point. Your Mormon friend, if he is up on his religion at all, believes in plurality of gods. He may even be very surprised that you don't.

To nail him down on plurality of gods, I ask leading questions. For example, I'll ask, "Do you agree with the statement, 'As man is, God once was; as God is, man may become'?" I have yet to have an active Mormon deny believing that.

You can ask, "Do you really believe you will be a god?" Again, you will probably have no trouble getting that admission.

It is important that you get your contact to commit to polytheism *before* you begin your philosophical or biblical discussion.

Second, demonstrate the philosophical basis for monothe-

ism. Mormonism would have us believe that Elohim was once a man and that he grew up on a planet and advanced to godhood. "God sits enthroned in yonder heavens an exalted man," Joseph Smith said. "He became God the same way all the other Gods before him."[11]

But think it through. Mormon theology makes it essential for all gods to have first been men. *So where did the first man come from?*

Notwithstanding the protests of Orson Pratt, that is the philosophical mistake of Mormonism—there is no *first* Father. There is, therefore, no Creator! No First Cause! In reality, there is no God as defined by any rational definition.

Joseph Smith's god who "found himself" in the beginning is not good enough. Where is the Creator? Joseph Smith said he had a doctrine calculated to exalt man:

> ...the soul—the mind of man—the immortal spirit. Where did it come from? All learned men and doctors of divinity say that God created it in the beginning; but it is not so: the very idea lessens man in my estimation.... The mind or the intelligence which man possesses is co-equal with God himself.[12]

Mormonism's failure is its inability to push itself back philosophically to the beginning.

God cannot have had a grandfather. Nothing can predate Him. Any being predating Him would *Himself* be God. God must be that Being beyond which no greater can be imagined. If something is bigger than your god, you are worshiping a demi-god.

When you do come to God, He stands alone. There is none like Him. We can never stress that too strongly. That is why God makes this concept the First Commandment: "Thou

11. *Journal of Discourses,* Vol. 6, pp. 1–7.
12. Smith, *Teachings of the Prophet Joseph Smith,* pp. 352-353.

shalt have no other gods beside me." That is the foundational revelation of God: "Hear, O Israel: The Lord, our God, the Lord is one" (Deuteronomy 6:4).

Third, demonstrate the biblical basis for monotheism. This part is easy. Once you have your contact thinking about the rational necessity for monotheism, you then open your Bible and quickly and decisively demonstrate the biblical monotheism. This is a telling moment because Mormons will tell you they believe the Bible is the Word of God, though they do not see it as infallible. Here's what you say:

"Let me show you just a few Scriptures that indicate monotheism in the Bible. I could go to any book in the Bible from Genesis 1:1 to Revelation 22:21, but I just want to read a few Scriptures from the book of Isaiah."

Then, without waiting for an answer, you open your Bible and start reading the following Scriptures. You will want to have them underlined.

"You are my witnesses," declares the Lord, "and my servant whom I have chosen, so that you may know and believe me and understand that I am he. Before me no god was formed, nor will there be one after me. I, even I, am the Lord, and apart from me there is no savior" (Isaiah 43:10–11).

This is what the Lord says—Israel's King and Redeemer, the Lord Almighty: I am the first and I am the last; apart from me there is no God. Who then is like me? Let him proclaim it (Isaiah 44:6–7).

When I'm talking to a Latter-day Saint, I say, "If He is the first and last, how many Gods are there?"

"You are my witnesses. Is there any God besides me? No, there is no other Rock; I know not one" (Isaiah 44:8).

"I am the Lord, and there is no other; apart from me there is no God . . . so that from the rising of the sun to the place

of its setting men may know there is none besides me. I am
the Lord, and there is no other" (Isaiah 45:5-6).

About this time your Mormon friend will be saying to
himself, "Well, obviously we are talking about the *god of
this world,* here." That means that the Mormon thinks that
Elohim or Jehovah (whoever is talking, and he won't be sure
which one is) is the god over the planet earth and no other.
When I see the "god of this planet" look in their eyes, I am
ready to proceed with Isaiah 45:12:

It is I who made the earth and created mankind upon it.
My own hands stretched out the heavens; I marshaled their
starry hosts.

That deals with the "god of this planet" theology. This
God, according to Job, binds the Pleiades and looses Orion
and brings forth all the other *constellations* in their season,
not just earth (see Job 38:31-33). We are talking about the
God who consistently claims to have created and to rule all
the heavens and all the stars: "Through him all things were
made" (John 1:3). "He stretches out the heavens like a can-
opy" (Isaiah 40:22).

For this is what the Lord says—he who created the heavens, he is God. . . . He says: "I am the Lord, and there is no
other. . . . There is no God apart from me. . . . There is none
but me. . . . I am God, and there is no other" (Isaiah
45:18-22).

Then I like to look them in the eye as I recite this last one:

"Remember this, fix it in mind, take it to heart, you rebels.
Remember the former things, those of long ago; I am God,
and there is no other; I am God, and there is none like me"
(Isaiah 46:8-9).

The reading of these Scriptures quickly and in order, with authority, is one of the most powerful experiences you will ever have witnessing to Mormons. The verses are so clear and powerful that they are devastating.

Your contact may try to interrupt you and sidetrack you. He may say, "That is talking about the god of this world."

I respond by saying, "The god of this world is the devil. We are talking about the Creator of the universe here. He says He created all the starry host. . . ." Then I just keep reading.

Talking About the Trinity

I love to talk to Mormons about the Trinity. The Trinity seems to be a frightening thing for most people. Maybe that's because they've been told so many times that you can't understand it. When I hear preachers say something glib like, "Well, the Trinity can't be understood, you just have to take it by faith," I get upset. One 74-year-old lady wrote me poignantly after listening to my tapes on the Trinity. "Why haven't we heard this before?" she asked. "We *can* understand it."

Of course we can't *fully* understand the Trinity. But that's no reason not to try. We can't understand electricity, and yet we train thousands of electricians every year. I was an electronics technician in the Navy. We were taught that nobody understands how electricity "flows." We didn't know if it flowed from positive to negative or from negative to positive. In fact, the best theories said the electrons didn't flow at all; rather the "holes" between the electrons flowed.

The doctrine of the Trinity, simply stated, is this: "In all the universe there is but one God and within the nature of the one God are Father, Son, and Holy Ghost."

Here's what we know about God from the Old Testament. He is one.

He is infinite.

He is eternal.

He is omniscient—He knows everything.

He is omnipotent—He is all-powerful.

He is omnipresent—He is present everywhere.

Only *after* we have the God of the Old Testament fixed in our minds are we able to move to the New Testament. And when we do, we are presented with Jesus. Of Him we read:

Jesus is omniscient (Revelation 2:18-19. John 1:48, 2:24).

Jesus is omnipotent (Revelation 1:18, 21:5-7, 22:12-13, 16.

Jesus is omnipresent (Matthew 18:20, 28:20).

Jesus is called God (John 1:1, 5:18, 10:30-33, 20:28; Colossians 2:9-10; 1 Timothy 3:16; Titus 2:12-13; Hebrews 1:8.)

Jesus is worshiped—an act reserved by Jews *only for the one true and living God* (Matthew 14:33, 15:25; Luke 24:52; John 9:38; Hebrews 1:6; Revelation 5:11-14).

Jesus is the Creator of all (John 1:3; Colossians 1:15-17; Hebrews 1:10).

After discovering that Jesus is God—that all the attributes of the Father are ascribed to Him—we then discover that, likewise, every attribute of God is reserved for the Holy Ghost as well!

Then I say to my Mormon friend: "Jesus said, 'Wherever two or three gather together in my name, there I am in the midst.' Do you believe Jesus is really here present with us?" (Had I asked him that earlier in the conversation he would have said no. But now, he almost always says yes.)

Then I ask: "If a prayer meeting were going on in China right now, do you think Jesus would be there?"

He usually says yes.

"What if there were a prayer meeting on Mars? Would Jesus be there? Or on a planet in another galaxy?

"See," I continue, "Jesus claims to be omnipresent." I use the passage from the King James Version, John 3:13. Jesus, talking to Nicodemus said, "No man hath ever ascended up

to heaven, [except] he that came down from heaven, even
the Son of man *which is in heaven* (KJV)." So Jesus was talking to Nicodemus and He "is in heaven."

The nature of God is the most difficult of all the foundational doctrines. But it is also the most rewarding. You will
see results more quickly talking about the nature of God
with a Mormon (after you have become sure of your own
theology) than you will in any other area. You may get
bogged down talking about salvation theory with a Mormon,
but I can promise you joy as you speak intelligently about
the nature of God.

In the next chapter I will give you the material to deal
with another great foundational stone: Revelation, both general and special. With a strong working knowledge in the
area of the nature of God and revelation, you will be ready
to talk solidly with any Mormon you encounter.

Chapter Nine

Revelation

"I am, or was, a Mormon. As I read [your book] I couldn't believe that someone else was going through the battle I am going through.

"My husband holds the Melchizedek Priesthood. . . . I have taught Spiritual Living Lessons. . . . We have been to the temple and had our two sons sealed to us.

"I know the Church is wrong. . . . There have been times I have wanted to take my own life. I had no one to talk to. All my old Mormon friends didn't want to listen to me. They said that Satan had hold of me.

"Then the Lord brought me some new friends that believe in Him. They fellowshiped with our family.

"I think I'm going to make it."

Bonnie

In the second century a young Persian boy named Mani, meditating in his backyard, was visited—so he said—by an angel who told him that he was "to restore the True Church." Little Mani's religion, Manicheaism, lasted 500 years, spread throughout the Roman Empire and garnered hundreds of thousands of converts.

Mani sent missionaries two by two throughout the Empire. They preached a legalistic gospel, changed the Bible and taught that exaltation came through a system of secret ceremonies.

One Manichean convert was a young law student named Augustine (eventually St. Augustine) who was a member of the cult for ten years before being born again reading the book of Romans.

Mani's story sounds somewhat like Joseph Smith's. So does the story of Mohammed, who, like Joseph and Mani, claimed to have been called to "restore the True Church." Mohammed said he was visited by the angel Gabriel and began, about 600 A.D., the religion of Islam, which today claims five hundred million adherents world-wide (there are about one hundred Muslims for every Mormon).

Both Joseph and Mani first shared their visions only with close family members. Mohammed's first converts were his wife and daughters, his cousin, his son-in-law, and his friend Aku-Bakr. After three years of private proselytizing he had forty followers and began to preach his doctrines publicly in Mecca.

There seems to be no end to the stream of new gurus—those whom "God has sent" to restore the old order or usher in a new one. Beginning with Simon the Sorcerer in the book of Acts, they parade down through the centuries. In the early centuries A.D. we had Mani, Sabellius, and Arius. The nineteenth century produced Joseph Smith, the Fox Sisters, Mary Baker Eddy, and Charles Taze Russell. And in our age we have had Jim Jones, Rajneesh, Victor Paul Wierwille, Sun Myung Moon, Herbert W. and Garner Ted Armstrong, and Elizabeth Claire Prophet, to name only a few. The list is endless. All these luminaries claim the mantle of the prophet of the restoration.

Peter warned us about these heretics:

> But there were also false prophets among the people,
> just as there will be false teachers among you. They will

secretly introduce destructive heresies.... Many will follow their shameful ways (2 Peter 2:1-2).

I never cease to be amazed that these false prophets seem to be able to seduce Christians without a great deal of trouble.

Why are Christians so vulnerable to the cults?

Paul says it is because we too easily put up with someone who preaches a "different" Jesus, a different spirit, or a different gospel (2 Corinthians 11:4).

Harold O. J. Brown, in his excellent book *Heresies,* says the reason lies not in the fact that Christians are fascinated with error, but in the fact that the fallen world system wants to "integrate Christ into its thinking without being profoundly changed by Him."[1] In other words, the false prophets want to add Christ to their mix so they can add Christians to their congregations.

Christians (God calls them sheep) follow strong-willed people who use the name of Christ to get control over them. That's why God charges shepherds to protect the sheep from wolves!

Objectivity vs. Subjectivity

False prophets come in among the sheep telling great spiritual lies. They display three characteristics.

First, they have false visions:

Do not let anyone who delights in false humility and the worship of angels disqualify you for the prize. Such a person goes into great detail about what he has seen, and his unspiritual mind puffs him up with idle notions (Colossians 2:18).

Second, they come *from within* the Christian Church:

1. Brown, p. 56.

They went out from us, but they did not really belong to us. For if they had belonged to us, they would have remained with us (1 John 2:19).

Third, they seek disciples:

I know that after I leave, savage wolves will come in among you and will not spare the flock. Even from your own number men will arise and distort the truth in order to draw away disciples after them (Acts 20:29–30).

False prophets worm their way in among the people and introduce their own thinking. They usually are men or women of charisma and warmth. People are attracted to them and, unfortunately, believe their unbiblical visions.

They often use the Bible to support their thinking, but *their own ideas* are most important.

And, mainly, they attempt to lead their followers into a subjective experience. They want them to "believe."

When Mormon missionaries, for example, present their gospel, they encourage listeners to strive for a spiritual experience to prove to themselves that Mormonism is true. They refer them to this passage in the Book of Mormon:

And when ye shall receive these things, I would exhort you that ye would ask God, the Eternal Father, in the name of Christ, if these things are not true; and if you shall ask with a sincere heart, with real intent, having faith in Christ, he will manifest the truth of it unto you, by the power of the Holy Ghost (Moroni 10:4).

Mormonism wants its converts to get a "feeling" (a "burning in the bosom") that the Book of Mormon is true. Mormonism wants its converts to begin to say four things:

—That they "know" that the Book of Mormon is "True."
—That they "know" Joseph Smith was a "True Prophet."

—That they "know" the Mormon Church is "God's True Church."

—That they "know" the President of the Church is a "Living Prophet of God."

All these points are based on a subjective feeling, a spiritual "knowing."

Jesus Is Different

Jesus Christ is unique among those who claim to come from God. He bases His divinity on *objective not subjective* concepts.

First, He fulfills numerous long-standing prophecies. His place of birth was prophesied hundreds of years in advance. His death a thousand years in advance (even the mode of execution—crucifixion—was stipulated, although crucifixion was not commonly practiced until five hundred years after the prophecy was written). Dozens of intricate Old Testament prophecies are exactly fulfilled in Christ, down to such specific details as the number of silver coins which would be paid for His betrayal.

Second, Jesus performed numerous miracles in the presence of thousands of people: raising the dead, opening congenitally blind eyes and ears, healing the sick everywhere He went, controlling the elements, defying natural laws by walking on water and through walls.

Third, He is resurrected. After His Resurrection from a sealed tomb guarded by Roman soldiers, He appeared throughout the countryside and was seen by hundreds of people—five hundred at one time. And the Jewish authorities, who had every reason to discredit the Resurrection (for example, by producing the dead body or charging the disciples with grave desecration and fraud), stand noticeably silent.

Jesus does not say, "Get a 'burning in your bosom' about Me." Rather, He says, "Test Me by the Scriptures."

To the Jews He said:

"You diligently study the Scriptures because you think
that by them you possess eternal life. These are the Scriptures that testify about me, yet you refuse to come to me to
have life" (John 5:39–40).

Again, on the road to Emmaus, He reprimanded the disciples for their unbelieving and unscriptural response to His
death and Resurrection:

He said to them, "How foolish you are, and how slow of
heart to believe all that the prophets have spoken! Did not
the Christ have to suffer these things and then enter his
glory?" And beginning with Moses and all the Prophets, he
explained to them what was said in all the Scriptures concerning himself (Luke 24:25–27).

*The difference between the testimony of Christ and the
testimony of Mormonism is the difference between objectivity and subjectivity.*

The Theory of Revelation

Revelation is God communicating with His creation. He
does it in two ways: through general revelation and through
special revelation. Let's look at these two forms of revelation
to see where Mormonism fits in, if at all.

General Revelation. The ancient Greek philosophers
looked at the universe and postulated a Creator. They said
some very specific things about His nature.
They said He was real.
Through their observance of natural order, they said He
was good.
This ability to perceive that God exists and that He is
good is called general revelation. The Bible indicates that

this revelation is available to all men. In fact, it is incumbent upon men to recognize, respect, and submit to the knowledge of God in general revelation.

As Psalm 19:1–4 says:

> The heavens declare the glory of God;
>   the skies proclaim the work of his hands.
> Day after day they pour forth speech;
>   night after night they display knowledge.
> There is no speech or language
>   where their voice is not heard.
> Their voice goes out into all the earth,
>   their words to the ends of the world.

Paul echoes these sentiments in Romans 1:19–20:

> What may be known about God is plain to [men], because God has made it plain to them. For since the creation of the world God's invisible qualities—his eternal power and divine nature—[the fact that He is and that He is good] have been clearly seen, being understood from what has been made, so that men are without excuse.

Special Revelation. After the Greek philosophers recognized the existence and goodness of God, they then made a wonderful philosophical leap. They said that a good God would not create a universe and populate it unless He planned to communicate with its inhabitants. By 200 B.C. the Greek philosophers fully expected that this good God would speak to men. They expected He would communicate His mind and will. The term the Greeks used for the mind and will of God was the word *logos* or "word." They said He would communicate His Word.

The apostle John used the concept of the *logos* in introducing Christ: "In the beginning was the Word [*logos*], and the Word was with God, and the Word was God" (John 1:1).

The specific communication of God's mind is called spe-

cial revelation. Another word for special revelation is prophecy. The Bible contains God's special revelation to mankind.

God has chosen to communicate specifically with mankind from the beginning. He spoke to Adam and Eve in the
Garden, with Noah during the time of the Flood, with Abraham and Moses and David and with all the prophets until
Christ. Hebrews 1:1-2 says it this way:

> In the past God spoke to our forefathers through the
> prophets at many times and in various ways, but in these
> last days he has spoken to us by his Son. . . .

And, of course, the Holy Spirit continued to speak through
the apostles and prophets after the death of Christ. The special revelation of God includes the Old Testament before
Christ and the New Testament after Christ.

Undermining the Bible

Any false prophet who wants to introduce unbiblical
practices among Christians must first undermine the authority of the Bible. That is exactly what Joseph Smith set out
to do. After Joseph Smith—occultist, visionary, and false
prophet—began to get a following among his friends and
family, one of his earliest accomplishments was to convince
people that the Bible was unreliable. He said his Book of
Mormon would unscramble what had been lost from the
Bible over the centuries. Even more important, he established his continuing revelations as the Word of God.

His church was the "Church of the Restoration" and the
Book of Mormon was the "Restoration of the Gospel" because "many plain and precious parts" of the Bible were de-
liberately taken away by the "great and abominable church,
the whore of all the earth" (I Nephi 13:26-29, 32, 40).

Undermining confidence in the Bible began early in Mormonism. Orson Pratt, the cream of the early Mormon schol-

ars, wrote books and pamphlets proving the Bible was unreliable. He said, "The Bible is not the word of God, but the word of uninspired translators":

> What evidence have [Protestants] that the book of Matthew was inspired by God, or any other of the books of the New Testament? . . . We all know that but a few of the inspired writings have descended to our times. . . . What few have come down to our day, have been mutilated, changed, and corrupted, in such a shameful manner that no two manuscripts agree. Verses and even whole chapters have been added by unknown persons. . . . Who knows that even one verse of the whole Bible has escaped pollution?[2]

Mormonism's Eighth Article of Faith states the official position:

> We believe the Bible to be the Word of God, as far as it is translated correctly; We also believe the Book of Mormon to be the Word of God.

Defending the Bible

One mistake evangelicals make is to get into a Bible discussion with Mormons without understanding that Mormonism does not see the Bible as the infallible Word of God. Although Mormons may *tell you* they believe the Bible is God's Word, in reality they *trust only the Mormon Church.*

What they believe will *not* be determined by what the Bible says. Their doctrine is dictated to them from the Church Office Building in Salt Lake City.

Until you bring them to judge the Mormon Church by the Bible, you are wasting your time.

To win Mormons, we must reinstate the Bible as the only rule for faith and doctrine.

2. *Orson Pratt's Works,* "The Bible Alone, an Insufficient Guide," pp. 44–47.

To do that, we must challenge the Mormon concept of revelation. Our goal is to get our Latter-day Saint friends to understand the following concept: *Former* revelation always judges *latter* revelation! Or to say it aother way, Latter-day revelation must be judged by the Bible.

What I am saying has its basis in a two-point foundation of logic:

First, if God speaks Scripture, that Scripture is true.

Second, since God doesn't change and since His Word endures forever, nothing He says will contradict what He previously said.

Our Mormon friends must understand that Joseph Smith is judged by the Bible, *not* vice versa. If we can bring the Mormon back to an inspired Bible, we will have eroded his dependence on his subjective experience. We will have begun the process of bringing him into objectivity.

Opening the Revelation Discussion

Here is the way I introduce the concept of revelation.

Me: God can't lie. What He says is true.

Mormon: Of course.

Me: For example, God led the children of Israel out of Egypt. One day Moses went up into the mountain and God told him, "Hear, O Israel: The Lord our God, the Lord is one!" You recognize that as Deuteronomy 6:4, do you not?

Mormon: Yes, that's correct.

Me: Now, Moses died. And Joshua led the children of Israel into the Promised Land. Can you imagine the reaction of the elders if Joshua were to go up into a mountain, have a revelation from God, come down and declare to the Israelites: "Hear, O Israel: The Lord, our God, the Lord is *two!*"? See, since God cannot lie, when He told Moses that God is one, He will not turn around and tell Joshua that God is two.

When I use this sequence with a Mormon I usually don't get a lot of resistance. One of the reasons is that I am not pressing the polytheism issue at this point. I am merely using the exchange to establish a logical sequence. And the logical sequence is really undeniable. Now the Mormon may later choose to argue with my term "God" and claim that while there may only be one god for this world, there are many others throughout the universe. But right now, I merely want to establish that God doesn't lie, change his mind, or correct Himself. I usually then come back with another similar example.

Me: Here's another example: God has declared He doesn't like adultery, right?

Mormon: Right.

Me: So if a so-called prophet comes along and says God told him adultery was okay, we would know God had *not* said it, right?

Mormon: Well, okay.

Me: My point is that *former revelation always judges latter revelation.* For example, Joshua couldn't get a valid revelation in direct contradiction with what Moses got. And David doesn't disagree with Joshua, and Elisha doesn't disagree with Elijah, and John and Paul and Peter don't disagree with Isaiah, Jeremiah, and Ezekiel.

At this point my LDS friend is about to object. He instinctively agrees that God doesn't change. But he has been taught otherwise. And, he still doubts that the Bible has been preserved correctly. While he is struggling, I say:

Me: In other words, because God doesn't change His mind, former revelation judges latter revelation, *assuming the former revelation has been accurately preserved.*

Now my Mormon friend readily agrees. My assumption has left him an escape. He believes the Book of Mormon corrects the Bible because the Bible has not been correctly preserved. If I can prove the Bible was not only *given* by the Holy Spirit, but also *preserved* by Him, then the Mormon's subjective confidence in the Book of Mormon may give way to faith in God's Word.

So now our job is to prove that the Bible *has* been preserved.

If we can accomplish that, we will have moved the Mormon from the labyrinth of subjective experience into objectivity. From that basis we can begin to examine the teachings of Mormonism in the light of the Bible. From there it is only a question of time. Only two options will remain for the Latter-day Saint. He can choose to change his belief system to line up with the Bible or he can choose to continue to adhere to a faith he no longer believes.

Proofs for the Preservation of the Bible

Our proof for the preservation of the Bible revolves around three concepts.

First is the futility of God giving Scripture if He knew it would be lost.

God spoke to man in Scripture. He was giving mankind a road map for living. He spoke to show us the way.

Since His speaking was a miraculous undertaking, the begging question is: *How could God start out to speak to man through Scripture and fail?* If God wanted to speak to mankind, to give his Scripture to the world, how is it that He only succeeded in giving it to one or two or a dozen generations?

It is logically inconsistent to think that the Creator could set out to give us Scripture and then be foiled in His attempt by the foibles of men. It is logically inconsistent to think that God sent His Scripture and men lost it. It is logically inconsistent to think that God inspired Scripture if he did not intend to preserve it.

Second is the vindication of the Old Testament by Christ.

A major proof of the accuracy of the Old Testament is that Jesus quoted from it copiously. He was satisfied that it had been faithfully preserved. He called it the Word of God. He read Hebrew and the Greek Septuagint. His confidence in the Old Testament gives us confidence in it.

Third is the science of textual criticism.

Textual criticism is the process by which scientists reconstruct the content of ancient documents. It is very simple in theory. Scientists simply gather together all the existing copies of an ancient document and compare them. *Our certainty of the content of the original is linked to the degree to which the copies agree.*

Of course, evangelical Christians have a high view of Scripture. We know that textual critics, whether they are Christian, Jew, Muslim, agnostic, or atheist, are in agreement regarding the miraculous preservation of the biblical text.

Latter-day Saints don't share that same high view of the Bible. I find, however, that many Mormons are interested in a simple, well-prepared apologetic for the accuracy of the Bible. Whenever possible I do what I call a "mini-course in textual criticism."

Mini-Course in Textual Criticism

My mini-course consists of four points and can be demonstrated in fifteen minutes in a coffee shop, by drawing on a napkin or the back of a placemat. It consists of four steps:

An overview of textual criticism.

The drawing of a simple chart.

The opinion of textual critics about the Bible.

An explanation of the process of preservation.

Step One: Overview of textual criticism.

I usually open with something like this:

"Throughout history, before the invention of the printing press, hand-copied books of the New Testament were carried throughout the Old World.

"Today scientists have access to thousands of these ancient manuscript fragments, which were found in various parts of the world—Africa, Asia, Europe.

"These documents were copied in various time periods. Some come to us from the eighth century, some from as early as the second century.

"A textual critic will assemble all the fragments of a particular portion of the New Testament and compare them to see if they agree or disagree."

Step Two: The chart.
Then I draw a chart, reproduced here as Chart C on page 107.

"This is a diagram of how copies of ancient documents come into our possession. For our example, let's take the book of Colossians. Chapter four, verse sixteen says, 'After this letter has been read to you, see that it is also read in the church of the Laodiceans.' (Colossae and Laodicea were two towns in what is now Turkey. Paul suggests that copies of his letters be passed around through the churches.)

"As time passed, more and more copies were made. The textual critic compares hundreds of fragments of the book of Colossians. If the copies vary widely, the textual critic will be uncertain about what the original said. But if the copies are in strict agreement, the textual critic knows, with a high degree of confidence, what the original said."

Then I stop talking and look at the Latter-day Saint. I'm ready for step three.

Step Three: The opinion of the textual critics.
If the system is working, my Mormon friend will ask what the textual critics say about the Bible text. When he asks that, reply:

CHART C
MANUSCRIPT COPIES USED IN TEXTUAL CRITICISM

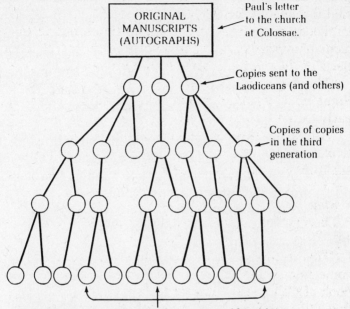

ORIGINAL MANUSCRIPTS (AUTOGRAPHS)

Paul's letter to the church at Colossae.

Copies sent to the Laodiceans (and others)

Copies of copies in the third generation

Multiple copies found in various centuries in Africa, Asia, and Europe are compared. Remarkable agreement demonstrates supernatural preservation.

"Well, textual critics, whether they are Christian, Jew, Muslim, or agnostic are in absolute agreement. They say that the text of the Bible is certain. One leading critic, Sir Frederic Kenyon, has said, 'It cannot be too strongly asserted that in substance the text of the Bible is certain.'[3]

"And *now*, even the Mormon Church is forced to agree. Dr. Richard Anderson, a BYU professor, says Kenyon is right! That all the ancient manuscripts agree in 99% of the

3. *Our Bible and the Ancient Manuscripts*, p. 23. For a comprehensive listing of statements for the authority of the Bible, see Josh McDowell's *Evidence That Demands a Verdict*, Vol. I, which discusses textual criticism clearly and fully, with heavy documentation.

Bible verses. And that there are no serious problems with the Bible.[4]

"So, we *know*—with amazing accuracy—what the apostle Paul wrote to the churches at Colossae and Rome and Philippi. Now, you'll have to decide if Paul was *inspired*—if what he wrote was the Word of God. That is a question of faith. But there is no doubt about *what* he said. We know that he wrote two thousand years ago to the church at Rome and Corinth and Philippi."

At this point, if the listener is with me, he is thinking that maybe God preserved the Bible after all. And now I want to give him some intellectual anchors to support this thinking. So I go into the fourth stage in my mini-course.

Step Four: The process of preservation.
God preserved His Word.
He said He would and He did.
But how did He do it?
He preserved His Word through the same agency He used to deliver it—men.

Joseph Smith was fond of saying that it was not unusual for "some old Jew" to change Scripture as he copied it. He implied that the Jewish copyists didn't respect the Word of God. However, nothing could be further from the truth. The New Testament writers, their colleagues, the early Church Fathers, and the men of God in all ages felt a divine reverence and respect for the Word of God. These men were willing, and often called, to die for merely *possessing* the books of the Bible.

The Old Testament scribes and scholars, Talmudists, believed it was their sacred duty to preserve the Scripture *exactly.* They believed they functioned under a divine calling and under the inspiration of the Holy Spirit in their work of transcription.

But, in addition to their feeling of spiritual anointing for

4. *Fourteenth Annual Symposium of the Archaeology of the Scriptures,* BYU, pp. 52–59.

their work, they devised intricate legal requirements for the work of copying. Talmudists adhered to the following regulations:[5]

—The scrolls had to be written on the skins of ceremonially clean animals.

—Every scroll had to contain a specific number of columns, each column a specific length and breadth. The scrolls were lined before they were written upon and any scroll with fewer than three words on a line was worthless (to prevent subsequent additions).

—The color and formula of the ink was specified.

—No word or mark could be written from memory; the scribe had to look at each word before he wrote it.

—Between each letter was the space of a hair's breadth or thread.

—The copyist had to sit in full Jewish dress.

—He must first wash his entire body.

—He could not begin to write the name of God with a pen newly dipped in ink, and should a king address him while writing that name, he must take no notice of him.

Any scrolls not produced according to these regulations were condemned to be buried or banished to the schools, to be used as reading primers.

As you can see, the Talmudists took their job seriously. This was the Word of God! No "old Jew" changed it at whim. The Bible was copied correctly over the centuries.

During the four hundred years from 500 A.D. to 900 A.D., a group of Jews called the Masoretes accepted the job of standardizing the Hebrew text. They produced what is known as the "Masoretic" Text, so reliable that virtually every modern translation—in all languages—relies exclusively upon it.

5. *The Hebrew Text of the Old Testament,* as cited in Josh McDowell, *Evidence that Demands a Verdict,* Campus Crusade For Christ, Arrowhead Springs, California, 1972, pp. 56–57.

They devised their own complicated system to ensure accuracy.[6]

—They numbered every verse, word, and *letter* of every book. In other words, if letter number 15,213 were wrong, they knew an error existed somewhere in the book and it was worthless.

—They calculated the middle letter of each book. If the middle letter of the copy were not the same as the original, the copy was not authentic. They also calculated the middle letter of the entire Old Testament.

—They set up other intricate formulae. For example, they recorded the total number of particular letters in many verses. So if a particular verse were to have seven "alephs" and had only six, the copy was invalidated.

The Jewish transcribers did a marvelous job. Their accomplishment was verified in a very unusual way in 1947 by the discovery of the Dead Sea Scrolls—rolls of parchment hidden away in a cave near the Dead Sea—marvelously preserved for two thousand years!

When the scholars examined these documents, they found that the Masoretic text had held up nearly perfectly. For example, of the 166 words of Isaiah 53, after one thousand years of copying, only three letters are in question, and those three letters do not affect the meaning of the text.

This is revelation. The fact that God has spoken to us. He gave us His Word. He preserved it, just as He said He would.

I call my Mormon friends to the enduring Word of God and away from subjective experience.

The Word of God is the objective yardstick by which Latter-day Saints may measure Joseph Smith, the Book of Mormon, and Mormon doctrine.

How hopeful it is to be able to tell our Mormon friends what the prophets, apostles, and God Himself has said:

6. McDowell, p. 58.

Your word, O Lord, is eternal; it stands firm in the heavens (Psalm 119:89).

"Heaven and earth will pass away, but my words will never pass away" (Mark 13:31).

"It is easier for heaven and earth to disappear than for the least stroke of a pen to drop out of the Law" (Luke 16:17).

You have been born again, not of perishable seed, but of imperishable, through the living and enduring word of God. For,
"All men are like grass,
    and all their glory is like the flowers of the field;
    the grass withers and the flowers fall,
        but the word of the Lord stands forever."
And this is the word that was preached to you (1 Peter 1:23–25).

Chapter Ten

The Book of Mormon

"I'm confused and need your guidance. I'm 29 years old, a wife and a mother.... My confusion comes from three of my bosses who are Mormons.... They are kind and helpful and seem so loving.

"I believe in Jesus. I know He died for my sins. I know there is only one God. So why am I being drawn into a tangled web of confusion by these people?

"Believe me, I need help!

"Am I slowly being brainwashed? Can these good people at work be devils in disguise?

"Please help me! Please write or call me soon."

Debbie

Dean Helland, who is now a Christian missionary to Chile, was raised in an offbeat Mormon sect (more than a hundred different splinter groups exist in the world of Mormonism). His family moved among the various Mormon communions, including the Reorganized Church of Jesus Christ of Latter Day Saints. Finally, his father, convinced that all the Mormon expressions were impure, moved Dean and the family to Arizona to "take the Book of Mormon to the Lamanites."

Dean's dad would take the family to a different Christian church each Sunday. Sometime during the service he would stand up and tell the congregation they needed the Book of Mormon if they were to be saved.

As a young man, Dean was convinced that the Book of Mormon was true. He "had a testimony of it." He challenged Christians to: "Show me one place where the Book of Mormon contradicts the Bible and I will lay down the Book of Mormon." He said no Christian ever accepted the challenge!

Dean was so certain that God was leading him to write a book in defense of the Book of Mormon that he began a minute comparison of the Book of Mormon and the Bible to prove that the Book of Mormon restored the *sense* of the Bible, the "plain and precious parts of the gospel" destroyed by the Catholic Church (as the Book of Mormon teaches in I Nephi 1:32, 40).

As Dean compared passages from Isaiah with their parallel in the Book of Mormon, he said, "I came across a verse that made my heart leap." He had discovered a place where the Book of Mormon clearly made sense out of an obscure verse of Isaiah.

The verse was Isaiah 2:9 (KJV), equivalent to II Nephi 12:9 (Utah version Book of Mormon). Here are the two verses side by side:

Bible
And the mean man boweth down, and the great man humbleth himself: therefore forgive them not.

Book of Mormon
And the mean man boweth *not* down, and the great man humbleth himself *not,* therefore, forgive him not.

What Dean saw was that the Book of Mormon corrected the sense of the Bible. Joseph Smith straightened out the Book of Isaiah. If mean men *don't* bow down or great men *don't* humble themselves, in the interests of justice, they should *not* be forgiven.

Dean left the verse elated. He returned to it a few days later to re-study it, "to savor the success of my discovery."

But this time, he saw the verses in context. He discovered that Isaiah was not talking about men who will not bow down to God; on the contrary, he was talking about men who *do bow down to idols!* God is saying, in this passage, "both small and great men are bowing down to idols and I won't forgive them for it."

Dean said, "It hit me like a bolt of lightning. Joseph Smith made a common mistake: *he failed to read in context.* He 'corrected' the Bible, assuming he knew better than the Holy Spirit. It was obvious that the Bible was the correct text, and the Book of Mormon was wrong."

Dean's story illustrates a principle and underscores the reason I like to talk about the Book of Mormon with my Mormon contacts. The principle is that *the Book of Mormon is one thing in Mormonism that can be approached objectively.*

It normally is *not* approached objectively, but subjectively, by Mormons. That is, Mormon proselytes are told to read the Book of Mormon, pray about it, and get a "feeling" about it. Many unwary people have approached the book looking for a spiritual experience and have found one! But truth is not an experience, no matter how sublime. On the other hand, people have spiritual experiences with tarot cards, ouija boards, the Koran, and Eastern mysticism of various forms.

Mormon leaders often speak about "a burning in the bosom." This expression is taken from *Doctrine and Covenants,* Section 9, verses 8-9, which is a prophecy given through Joseph Smith to Oliver Cowdery during the "translating" of the Book of Mormon. Oliver is told that the translation process works this way:

> You must study it out in your mind; then you must ask me
> if it be right, and if it is right I will cause that your bosom

shall burn within you; therefore you shall feel that it is right.

When Mormon missionaries are teaching those who investigate Mormonism, they ask them to read the Book of Mormon and then pray about whether or not it is from God. They "bear their testimonies" that they have read the book and that they "know by the power of the Holy Ghost" that it is true. Then they have the investigator read Moroni 10:4 and seek their own "feeling":

> And when ye shall receive these things, I would exhort you that ye would ask God, the Eternal Father, in the name of Christ, if these things are not true; and if you shall ask with a sincere heart, with real intent, having faith in Christ, he will manifest the truth of it unto you, by the power of the Holy Ghost.
> And by the power of the Holy Ghost ye may know the truth of all things (Moroni 10:4, 5).

This is a particularly insidious proposal. It sounds so spiritual. Here is a person who is seeking God. He is told that if he follows this formula that he will have a "spiritual experience."

The problem is twofold. First, God is not into burning-bosom formulas. He has not said in Scripture that He will give you a burning in the bosom to tell you if something is true. Hearing from God is a rather fine spiritual process. As a counselor and pastor I find that young Christians have difficulty hearing from God. It takes time, it takes confirmation from Scripture, it takes godly counsel from proven brothers and sisters to know God's will.

But the Mormon missionaries say it is a "spiritual experience." And one that a novice can have with absolute confidence that he will not hear a counterfeit voice. This is terribly dangerous counsel. And it is exactly how Joseph Smith got into trouble in the first place.

These subjective ideas form the foundation for the Mormon experience. But if one allows himself to equate "experience" with truth, he isolates himself from reason and from Scripture.

The second problem is that *contained within the Book of Mormon are passages plagiarized from the Bible.* Whole chapters, indeed, whole sections are copied. These passages are, in fact, Scripture. They are true. That means packaged within the fraudulent Book of Mormon are sections of genuine Scripture. So, the question becomes, "What is the person investigating Mormonism praying about when he asks for a 'testimony' as to the validity of the Book of Mormon?" Is he praying about the parts that are true? Or is he praying about the whole thing?

Of the "burning in the bosom," Ed Decker, former Mormon and founder of "Saints Alive!", says he remembers his chest actually feeling ten degrees hotter than the rest of his body when he prayed about the Book of Mormon. But he goes on to say that he has also had a burning in his bosom from pizza. And from a crush he had on Susy Smith!

Religious truth cannot be documented by "spiritual experience" because the dark side to spiritual power is capable of appearing as light. As Paul says:

> False apostles, deceitful workmen [are] masquerading as apostles of Christ. And no wonder, for Satan himself masquerades as an angel of light. It is not surprising, then, if his servants masquerade as servants of righteousness (2 Corinthians 11:13–15).

Joseph Smith said an angel appeared to him to guide him to the Book of Mormon. That may be true. That is, he may have had an experience with a spirit being. Personally, I think he did. But I think the power Joseph contacted was evil. I think he spoke with demons. We know he was heavily involved with the occult (see Chapter Three). So it's reasonable to expect he would have contact from the spirit world. But God has warned us against occult experimentation because *Satan is a liar.*

Joseph should have checked the *message* of the angel against the gospel of Christ: "But even if we or an angel from heaven should preach a gospel other than the one we preached to you, let him be eternally condemned!" (Galatians 1:8).

We don't judge truth by demonstrations of spiritual pyrotechnics:

> The coming of the lawless one will be in accordance with the work of Satan displayed in all kinds of counterfeit miracles, signs and wonders, and in every sort of evil that deceives those who are perishing. They perish because they refused to love the truth and so be saved. For this reason God sends them a powerful delusion so that they will believe the lie (2 Thessalonians 2:9–11).

Mormons base their faith in the fact that Joseph Smith received the Book of Mormon from God. The Book of Mormon is *central* to the Mormon's faith. A young Latter-day Saint told me he could give up Joseph Smith and remain a Mormon; he could, if necessary, abandon Mormon theology; his faith could even stand the thought of current Mormon leaders going wrong. But, he said, "If I ever found out that the Book of Mormon were not given by God, I could not remain a Mormon."

I believe the Book of Mormon invites objective study.

I believe it is a tangible handle by which we can grasp the deception of Mormonism.

And most important, I think it is relatively easy to demonstrate that the Book of Mormon cannot be what the Mormon Church has said it is.

The Book of Mormon may indeed be "the key to conversion." Honest Mormons—when they find the Book of Mormon to be full of inconsistencies and errors—may turn from Mormonism.

Joseph's Story

Joseph Smith claimed that God had appeared to him in a vision and told him to restore the True Church. Joseph was then to wait until he received further instruction.

That instruction came when he began receiving late-night visits from a spirit calling himself "Moroni," who claimed to have been a soldier of the white-skinned Nephites, former inhabitants of the North American continent.

The Nephites, Moroni supposedly said, were descendants of a Jew named Lehi, who left Jerusalem with his family to escape the destruction of Jerusalem about 600 B.C. Under the direction of God, this family constructed small covered boats and sailed to the New World, landing in South or Central America.

Some of the descendants of Lehi were evil and God cursed them with a dark skin. These became the progenitors of the American Indians.

The more righteous descendants of Lehi, Nephites, warred against the unrighteous descendants, Lamanites, and were driven eastward across North America to western New York where Moroni buried gold plates containing the records of his people.

Now Moroni said that God had directed him to return to the earth and deliver the plates to Joseph, who would be enabled to translate and publish them as the Book of Mormon. (After publication, the plates were conveniently taken back into heaven.)

Two affidavits were bound into the front of the Book of Mormon when it was published in 1830: The Testimony of the Eight Witnesses and the Testimony of the Three Witnesses. Both these documents swore to the authenticity of the Book of Mormon. (Mormon apologists seldom mention that all Three Witnesses and all of the Eight Witnesses—except the Smiths—fell out with Joseph Smith and left the Church. One of the witnesses, Martin Harris, later rejoined the Church.)

Exposing the Book of Mormon

Sadly, the fact is that the Book of Mormon is a fraud—there never were any gold plates. Millions have been taken in by Joseph's deception. Our job is to rescue all we can from the deception. There are several ways the Book of Mormon can be demonstrated to be of human, not divine, origin.

First, the changes in the Book of Mormon. The Book of Mormon was said to have been translated "by the gift and power of God" and is "the most perfect of any book on the face of the earth." But, the fact that it has been changed some 4,000 times in the last 150 years demonstrates it is of human, not divine, origin.

Second, the theology of the Book of Mormon. The Book of Mormon was given to restore "plain and precious things" lost from the Bible. But the theology of the Book of Mormon does not support much of the theology of Mormonism. In fact the Book of Mormon actually *opposes* at times the theology of the Mormon Church. If Mormonism does not teach the Book of Mormon, then either the Book of Mormon is wrong or the Church itself is apostate.

Third, the archaeology of the Book of Mormon. The Book of Mormon supposedly is "a history of the ancient inhabitants of this continent." But the sciences of geography, archaeology, and anthropology demonstrate the Book of Mormon cannot be a record of pre-Columbian American peoples.

In spite of all the testimony of good, faithful Mormons, and in spite of the fact that I, myself, for ten years believed the Book of Mormon to have been given by God, I must say that *anyone* who will look at the book objectively (instead of subjectively) can see it is a fabrication!

I agree with the conclusions of the Rev. M. T. Lamb, who wrote *The Golden Bible* published in 1887. Lamb said:

> After a very careful study of the book, a conscientious and painstaking examination of all the evidences . . . for and against it . . . [I] am compelled to believe: that no such people as are described in the Book of Mormon ever lived upon this continent; that no such records were ever engraved upon golden plates . . . ; that no such men as Mormon or Moroni . . . ever existed in this country; that Jesus Christ never appeared upon this continent in person, or had a people here before its discovery by Columbus . . . [that] the book is . . . a . . . fabrication without any foundation in fact—that had its origin, simply and solely, in the brain or brains of men in our own day, without any help from God or from an angel from God (pages 11–12).

Problems and Changes in the Text of the Book of Mormon

Joseph and his friends who acted as scribes in translating the Book of Mormon were poorly educated. They couldn't spell and their grammar was bad. Although Joseph claimed to translate by the "gift and power of God," the result was very human as evidenced by these examples:

> . . . These our dearly beloved brethren, who have so dearly beloved us (Alma 26:9; 1830 edition, p. 296).
> . . . Yea, if my days could have been in them days . . . But, behold, I am consigned that these are my days (Helaman 7:8–9; 1830 edition, p. 427).
> . . . And they having been waxed strong in battle, that they might not be destroyed (Alma 9:22; 1830 edition, p. 247).
> . . . Even until we had arriven to the land of Middoni (Alma 20:30; 1830 edition, p. 282).

The only passages spelled correctly and correct grammatically, are the chapters of Isaiah Joseph lifted whole out of the King James Bible. The King James passages are, in fact, verbatim, proving that Joseph did not translate them from reformed Egyptian hieroglyphics as he claimed. Joseph so faithfully plagiarized the King James passages that he even included the italicized words in the text—*the transitional words the King James translators added for clarity, but which were not in the Hebrew text.*

Some of the sentences Joseph constructed were nearly four hundred words long, rambling, nearly incomprehensible repetitions of meaningless verbiage. In contrast, Jesus' Sermon on the Mount includes eighteen complete, meaningful sentences in the first three hundred and forty words. The most complex sentence in the New Testament does not reach 100 words and is clear and readable. Compare the clarity and beauty of the Bible with these sentences from the early Book of Mormon:

> ... And thus we see that they buried their weapons of peace, or they buried their weapons of war, for peace (Alma 24:19; 1830 edition, p. 292).
> ... They being shielded from the more vital parts of the body, or the more vital parts of the body being shielded from the strokes of the Lamanites (Alma 43:38; 1830 edition, p. 343).
> ... There were no robbers, nor murderers, neither were there Lamanites, nor any manner of ites; but they were one, the children of Christ (IV Nephi 1:17; 1830 edition, p. 515).
> ... Now immediately when the Judge had been murdered; he being stabbed by his brother by a garb of secrecy; and he fled, and the servants ran and told the people (Helaman 9:6; 1830 edition, p. 431).
> ... He went forth among the people, waving the rent of his garment in the air, that all might see the writing which he had wrote upon the rent. (This one was fixed up in recent editions as Alma 46:12–19; 1830 version, p. 351).

Many ludicrous passages remain unchanged in the Book of Mormon. For example, the book of Jacob ends with a French word:

> I make an end of my writing upon these plates, which writing has been small; and to the reader I bid farewell, hoping that many of my brethren may read my words. Brethren, *adieu*.

Adieu? How could a French word be translated from Reformed Egyptian into English? And *why*?

My favorite of all the scenes in the Book of Mormon closes the book of Ether (not, of course, so named for its effect on the reader, although Mark Twain referred to the Book of Mormon as "chloroform in print." He also said that if you took out all of the "and it came to pass" phrases, there would be nothing left to come to pass!).

Ether ends with a scene in which Coriantumr kills a man by the name of Shiz by "smiting off his head." Ether 15:31 says that after his head was smitten off, Shiz rose up on his hands and struggled for breath and died. Now, how can a body, separated from its head, rise up on its hands and struggle for breath? This sounds more like a line from the Mikado than from Holy Writ!

The Church has corrected many of the glaring errors of the book in subsequent editions over the past 150 years and many of the 4000 changes in Joseph Smith's original are in this category. Not all of these changes were simply grammatical, however, and cannot be laid simply to "typos." (As B. H. Roberts, prominent Mormon historian, says, "The first edition of the Book of Mormon is singularly free from typographical errors." Rather, he says, the errors in the Book of Mormon are "constitutional in nature."[1]

1. *Defense of the Faith,* B. H. Roberts, p. 280–281, reprinted in Francis W. Kirkham, *A New Witness for Christ in America,* Vol. 1, pp. 200-201.

Some of the changes involve important *doctrinal* changes, reflecting evolving Mormon doctrine. They are attempts to "fix" the Book of Mormon so it would fit in with new Mormon doctrine. For example, Joseph's concept of the nature of God underwent radical revision between 1830 and his death in 1844. Smith's early, unformed theology, as it appears in the Book of Mormon, is a patchwork exposing an immature concept of the nature of God that appears to be a form of Unitarianism.

If you were forced to nail down the Book of Mormon theology about God, you might choose to call it Modalism (one God who appears sometimes as the Father, sometimes as the Son, as in Mosiah 15:1-4). The doctrine of the Holy Spirit in the Book of Mormon—as it remains in the Mormon Church today—is particularly unclear. (See Appendix A: "The Book of Mormon and the Nature of God.")

One thing is certain, however. The Book of Mormon is *not* polytheistic. There is not even a *hint* that men may become gods!

As Joseph Smith's theology evolved he began to explain the Persons of the Godhead as "separate and distinct personages." Soon he was tri-theistic—he had three separate gods. Eventually in spite of the Book of Mormon he became a full-blown polytheist.

As his theology changed, the 1830 Book of Mormon theology became obsolete and needed to be changed. Some of the Trinitarian-sounding passages have been cleverly reworded to completely change their meanings.

In the following four examples, the underlined words have been added since the 1830 version was published. These passages come from a vision given to a man named Nephi in the Book of Mormon. In the original they say: "The virgin is the mother of God; the Lamb of God is the Eternal Father; and the Everlasting God was judged by the world." They have been changed by adding the words "the Son of" in appropriate places to change radically the meaning of the text (quoted below from the 1830 edition):

Behold, the virgin whom thou seest, is the mother of the Son of God, after the manner of the flesh (I Nephi 11:18, p. 25).

And an angel said to me, "Behold, the Lamb of God, yea, even the Son of the Eternal Father!" (I Nephi 11:21, p. 25).

The Son of the Everlasting God was judged of the world; and I saw and bear record (I Nephi 11:32, p. 26).

These last records ... shall make known to all kindreds, tongues, and people, that the Lamb of God is the Son of the Eternal Father, and the Savior (I Nephi 13:40, p. 32).

Jerald and Sandra Tanner in their work *3,913 Changes in the Book of Mormon* document specific changes. Not only has the Book of Mormon been changed, but so has the book *Doctrine and Covenants*. In fact, it has been changed *more* than the Book of Mormon. The process of change continues to this day. After the 1978 "revelation" that blacks could hold the priesthood, II Nephi 30:6 in the Book of Mormon was changed. It used to say that Lamanites (the supposed dark-skinned forerunners of the American Indians) became "white and delightsome" when they accepted the Mormon gospel. But after the priesthood revelation, the text was changed to say they became "pure and delightsome." (I can remember hearing Mormon leaders say that when American Indians joined the Church their skin slowly got lighter.)

Even though the Book of Mormon has been changed thousands of times, it remains clearly unpolytheistic while the Church doctrine is clearly polytheistic. *Therefore, the central theology of the Book of Mormon is in direct opposition to the theology of the Church.*

The Fall of the Book of Mormon

As attention continues to focus on the Book of Mormon, its viability as a historical document flags. Brigham Young

University anthropologists and archaeologists are challenging the historicity of the book. For example, BYU Professor of Anthropology Ray T. Matheny calls the constant reference in the Book of Mormon to iron implements "a king-size problem":

> The Book of Mormon talks about ferrous and non-ferrous metallurgical industries. A ferrous industry is a whole system of doing something. It's just not an esoteric process that a few people are involved in, but ferrous industry ... means mining iron ores and then processing these ores and casting [them] into irons.... This is a process that's very complicated ... it also calls for cultural backup to allow such an activity to take place.... In my recent reading of the Book of Mormon, I find that iron and steel are mentioned in sufficient context to suggest that there was a ferrous industry here....[2]

But Matheny says archaeology proves that there was no iron mining in the Western Hemisphere in pre-Columbian times. And there is no room for making a mistake about it:

> You can't refine ore without leaving a bloom of some kind or ... impurities that blossom out and float to the top of the ore ... and also the flux of limestone or whatever is used to flux the material.... [This] blooms off into silicas and indestructible new rock forms. In other words, when you have a ferroused metallurgical industry, you have these evidences of the detritus that is left over. You also have the fuels, you have the furnaces, you have whatever technologies that were there performing these tasks; they leave solid evidences. And they are indestructible things.... No evidence has been found in the new world for a ferrous metallurgical industry dating to pre-Columbian times. And so this is a king-size kind of problem, it seems to me, for the so-called Book of Mormon archaeology. This evidence is absent.[3]

2. Ray T. Matheny, Speech at Sunstone Symposium 6, "Book of Mormon Archaeology," Aug. 25, 1984.
3. Matheny.

The Book of Mormon not only mentions iron, but steel and machinery and scimitars and breastplates and metal engraving (which calls for hardened steel-tipped tools to chase metal). It speaks of gold and silver coinage—no Western-style coins have ever been found from pre-Columbian America.

The Book of Mormon mentions shipbuilding, sailing, the use of the magnetic compass, wheeled vehicles (drawn by horses), tent manufacture, and linen manufacture. Archaeologists unanimously agree that none of these activities took place in the New World before the arrival of the Spanish colonizers. The Book of Mormon also describes non-Western agricultural products like wheat and barley, flax and vineyards (and wine presses). These are giant archaeological problems. So is the description of domestic animals such as dogs, cows, goats, sheep, horses, asses, oxen, swine, and elephants. In addition the Book of Mormon uses attending cultural backup words like: pasture, chariot, stable, horned cattle, fowl, lamb, and fatlings.

Matheny concludes that the Book of Mormon terminologies and language are "nineteenth-century literary concepts and cultural experiences one would expect Joseph Smith and his colleagues to experience." In other words, this Brigham Young University professor thinks Joseph Smith made up the Book of Mormon.

Another BYU Professor, John L. Sorensen, an anthropologist, says the American Indians clearly *did not* descend from Hebrews; the languages of the New World *do not* have a Hebrew root; and the physical and biological characteristics of the American Indians *are not* Semitic. (The American Indians are, with no challenge, Mongoloid, not Caucasian. No amount of breeding will produce Mongoloids from Caucasians.)

Sorensen also says there is no way the geography spoken of in the Book of Mormon could have stretched thousands of miles from South America to New York—as the Book of

Mormon states. "It could not have been longer than seven hundred miles," Sorensen says. Latter-day Saints, according to Sorensen, are going to have to revise their concept of truth about the Book of Mormon.

A Mormon Giant Who Lost Confidence in the Book of Mormon

Brigham H. Roberts was a Mormon General Authority, historian, and apologist who wrote the six-volume Mormon history, *Comprehensive History of the Church*. Nearly all Mormons are familiar with and respect Roberts. But most of them do not know of his battle to maintain belief in the Book of Mormon. A battle that he lost.

Toward the end of his life Roberts reexamined the Book of Mormon and concluded that it was not of divine origin. He decided Joseph Smith could have, and probably had, plagiarized the ideas and much of the material from existing works and from his own imagination. I have set forth the details of Robert's fall from faith in Appendix B at the back of this book.

The Spalding Theory

One of the persistent theories is that Joseph Smith plagiarized the Book of Mormon from a "romantic novel" written by a Congregational minister prior to 1812. (I have appended the basics of this theory in Appendix C.) Solomon Spalding supposedly wrote two such stories: a short one, now on display at Oberlin College, and a larger one, now lost.

One version of the Spalding Theory is that Sidney Rigdon, a Baptist/Campbellite preacher of some disrepute and an early Mormon leader, stole the Spalding manuscript from a print shop and conspired with Smith to "bring it forth."[4]

Another obvious source document for the Book of Mormon is Ethan Smith's *View of the Hebrews.*

However the Book of Mormon came to be, I believe it is a most fertile field of study for those who would lead Latter-day Saints to Christ. Here we can grapple with real inconsistencies—not shadows of the past—both internal and external to the text.

If we can get Latter-day Saints to look at the history of the Book of Mormon, and to examine its text in the light of the Bible, we are on our way to winning them.

4. See *Who Really Wrote the Book of Mormon?,* Wayne L. Cowdrey, Howard A. Davis and Donald R. Scales, Vision House, Santa Ana, 1977.

Chapter Eleven

How to Answer Mormon Questions

> "As I read your book, the strangest feeling came over me because I realized that you had put into words the very thoughts and uneasy feelings I had always had.... I wanted to ask questions, but I always thought there was some unworthiness in me that made me feel like I wasn't good enough....
>
> "One day during a talk with my Christian friend ... [she told me that] Jesus loved me. I couldn't see how Jesus could possibly love a sinner like me, but she was so sincere in what she said that it brought tears to my eyes....
>
> "I accepted Jesus as my personal Savior in March and I now have the peace, comfort, and joy that only the Lord can give."
>
> **Janice**

Often Christians find themselves suddenly in very esoteric conversations with Latter-day Saints. The Mormon is eager—and well-prepared—to discuss subjects totally unfamiliar to the Christian. The Mormon, for example, may begin to talk about "baptism for the dead," an obscure, unscriptural rite practiced by Mormons.

There is no reason for a Christian to have a thought about baptism for the dead. It's not a doctrine of the Christian

Church; we cannot alter the condition of the dead. Yet suddenly, your friend is quoting a Scripture out of context (actually Paul is talking about the dead being raised to life): "What shall they do which are baptized for the dead, if the dead rise not at all?" (see 1 Corinthians 15:29).

You stutter and stammer and try to bring yourself up to speed. You know *something* is wrong, but you're not sure what. It's a frustrating experience.

Worse, as you fumble along *on the railroad track the Mormon has chosen,* you look foolish and the Latter-day Saint becomes further convinced that Mormonism has all the answers.

I have seen young Christians won to Mormonism because they got into discussions in these esoteric areas and couldn't think their way through them fast enough. *As a matter of fact, this is the fundamental tactic of the cults: Overpower the prospect with a barrage of information that is out of context and flawed in reasoning.* The prospect—unprepared to deal with the diabolically packaged doctrine—becomes impressed with the "logic" of it all. The cultist is confident and moves smoothly through his flip chart or prepared presentation, refuting any objections that may arise. It's a terribly effective and sinister program.

Our only response is to prepare ourselves in advance. To think through *in context* the passages of Scripture. To prepare reasonable answers. To speak to the error with truth and authority.

I could not, in this book, cover every subject that might come up. Only experience will prepare you for that. But I can show you the process, the art of dialoging with cultists: resisting easy answers to complex problems; discussing the presuppositions; reading every passage in the context; and of course, *isolating, qualifying, and verifying.*

I want to show you how I answer specific questions posed by my Mormon friends. I have prepared answers to nine common questions asked by Latter-day Saints. I answer the first question in rather complete detail, giving you the feeling for the dialogue. Thereafter I'm more concerned with giving you information and suggesting key phrases you can deliver at your own pace.

1. Why Do You Tell People We Aren't Christians?

The Mormon who asks this will go on to say that "the very name of our Church declares we are 'The Church of Jesus Christ.' " He may even say, "I believe in Jesus Christ. I'm as much of a Christian as you are!"

Here's how I respond:

"What would you say if I told you I am really a Mormon?"

"Well, I'd say you are lying, you're not a Mormon."

"No, really, I am. I'm a Mormon, I just don't believe in the Book of Mormon."

"What do you mean?"

"Well, I'm a Mormon, but I don't think Joseph Smith was a prophet. In fact, I don't think he had any of the visions he said he had. I think he was a fraud. . . . But, I'm a Mormon."

"That's ridiculous!"

"No, I'm a Mormon, although, I must admit, I don't believe men can become gods. I don't believe in the Mormon priesthood, I don't believe in temple work or that you have to be baptized to be saved . . ."

"Well, you are absolutely *not* a Mormon, then."

"Are you telling me that I can only be a Mormon if I believe what Mormons believe. . . ?"

By this time, of course, my friend is getting the point. So I drive the point home this way:

"Obviously, I really am *not* a Mormon—because I don't believe what Mormons believe. If I went around telling people I was a Mormon, they would have the right to assume I believe what Mormons believe. When Mormons who do not believe what Christians believe go around telling people they're Christians, the *real* Christian community has the responsibility to challenge them."

I might then go on to tell my Mormon friend that Paul in 2 Corinthians 11:4 talks about false apostles who preach a different Jesus, a different spirit, and a different gospel:

—The Jesus of Mormonism is the "spirit-brother" of Satan; the Jesus of Christianity *created* Satan.

—The spirit of Mormonism is occult in nature, as evidenced by the temple ceremony (see *Beyond Mormonism*) and polytheism.

—The Gospel of Jesus is salvation by grace through faith; the gospel of Mormonism is salvation by good works.

"Therefore," I say, "Mormonism has a different Jesus, a different spirit, and a different gospel. It's my responsibility to point that out."

2. Why Are You Attacking My Church?

"I'm not attacking your church. I'm not attacking anything or anybody. I'm expressing my opinion on a subject I think is important. This is America, the place where everybody is free to express his religious viewpoint—even when it is unpopular.

"I defend the right of Mormon missionaries to go door to door attempting to win Protestants and Catholics to Mormonism. But, in the interest of fairness, I claim the same right."

I then go on to say that today nearly 30,000 Mormon missionaries are talking to Baptists, Methodists, Pentecostals, Presbyterians—telling them that their pastors and priests do not have the authority to baptize or administer Sacraments. They say they need to leave their churches and join the Mormon Church.

"You want people to listen to the Mormon message. Well, I want people to listen to *my* message: Mormonism is wrong.

You don't have to become a Mormon to please God. As a matter of fact, I think you will *dis*please God by becoming a Mormon. I think you'll *alienate* yourself from God by joining the Mormon Church. The Mormon Church is not God's True Church. In fact, in my opinion, Mormonism is not even *a* true church. Basically, Mormonism, by its ungodly doctrine of polytheism, has disqualified itself from consideration as a Christian Church.

"And remember, we Christians are *defending* ourselves against Mormonism, not *attacking* it. Joseph Smith threw down the gauntlet when he said, 'All other denominations are wrong, all their creeds are abominations and all the professors of those creeds are corrupt.'[1]

"You Mormons are offended when someone says Mormonism is unchristian, but *at this very moment, as we speak, in Mormon temples throughout the world, Protestant ministers are portrayed as hirelings of Satan who only preach for money!"* (If I really want to drive my point home I will ask, *"Isn't that true?"*)

"It's hard for me to understand how Mormonism can work so hard to get people to leave Protestant and Catholic churches and then be so upset when we answer back.

"Thirty thousand Mormon missionaries work full-time to spread Mormonism; only a handful of Christians are attempting to counteract that Mormon effort."

3. Where Do You Get Your Authority?

The Mormon means *priesthood* authority by this. He believes in a priesthood that Jesus conferred upon the apostles, who passed it on to others.

This belief centers in the fact that Jesus chose twelve to establish, His work. And He had an ordination ceremony

1. *Pearl of Great Price*, Joseph Smith 2:19.

where He "laid hands" on them. At the death of Judas, the eleven gathered together and cast lots to fill the vacancy and bring the number of apostles back up to twelve.

Mormonism teaches that after the death of Jesus, the apostles became separated and were killed. They didn't have the chance to get together and keep the "quorum" of apostles full. Therefore the church was lost from the face of the earth. The authority of God was "restored" when Peter, James, and John appeared to ordain Joseph Smith to the Melchizedek Priesthood. He, in turn, named the other eleven apostles. Today, the missionaries say, when a Mormon apostle dies, the Quorum of Twelve Apostles must meet and fill the vacancy. (Oddly enough, this actually is *not* always done.)

I see several flaws in the reasoning behind Mormon priesthood theology. I think it's one of the weakest positions in Mormonism. Let's take it a step at a time:

First, if Joseph Smith could ordain ten or eleven other apostles, why couldn't any *one* of the original twelve do the same thing? It makes no difference how separated they got from each other. If Joseph can do it by himself, or with Oliver Cowdrey, why couldn't Andrew or James?

Second, just because it was done once to replace Judas, in the first chapter of Acts, that does not establish it as a precedent for every subsequent case. There is no other mention of this "quorum ordination" in the Bible, and Paul later names apostleship as one of the gifts of the Spirit, indicating apostles are not labeled so solely by the vote of the rest of the apostles.

Third, the New Testament doesn't set the continual number of apostles at twelve. In fact, the New Testament calls several other people apostles besides the twelve—men who lived at the same time as the twelve: Barnabas (Acts 14:3–4, 14); Andronicus and Junias (Romans 16:7); Silas and Timothy (1 Thessalonians 1:1; 2:6); James, the Lord's brother (not one of the original Twelve, Galatians 1:19); even Christ is referred to as an apostle. (Hebrews 3:1).

Fourth, Paul goes to great lengths to say that he was *not* ordained an apostle by a quorum (Romans 1:5; 1 Corinthians 1:1; 2 Corinthians 1:1).

In Galatians 1:1 he says he is an apostle "sent not *from* men nor *by* man." He says he wasn't even taught the Gospel by men, much less a church organization: "I did not receive it from any man, nor was I taught it; rather, I received it by revelation from Jesus Christ" (Galatians 1:12).

Paul says that when he received the Gospel, he didn't even talk to any of the church leaders about it:

> I did not consult any man, nor did I go up to Jerusalem to see those who were apostles before I was.... After three years, I went up to Jerusalem to get acquainted with Peter and stayed with him fifteen days. I saw none of the other apostles—only James, the Lord's brother (Galatians 1: 16–19).

It was fourteen years before this most singular apostle returned to Jerusalem to talk to others:

> As for those who seemed to be important—whatever they were makes no difference to me; God does not judge by external appearance—those men added nothing to my message. On the contrary they saw that I had been given the task of preaching the gospel to the Gentiles (Galatians 2:6–7).

This hardly seems like a man who was operating as a member of a monolithic church that made its moves by quorum decision. The unity of the Church of Christ is by the Spirit, not by legislation. The mistake Mormons make is they do not understand that the real mystery of God is that "Christ [is] in us, the hope of glory." We *are* a royal priesthood—all those of us who are believers in Him.

The entire book of Hebrews is dedicated to the proposition that a narrow, limited priesthood ended with Jesus and that now, all believers share the same priesthood because of their faith in Christ.

4. How Did Jesus Pray to Himself in the Garden of Gethsemane?

This is an attack on the biblical concept of the holy Trinity. Christians believe that there is only one God, and within the nature of that one God are three eternal Persons who exist without confusion and without separation.

I discuss the Trinity in more detail in Chapter Eight, but on the question of Jesus in Gethsemane I say,

"God is all-powerful and can manifest Himself in three places at once (or three thousand). He is omnipresent, in an infinite number of places at once. He can appear as a burning bush or a pillar of cloud—or as 'a wheel within a wheel' or as one with a double-edged sword coming out of nis mouth."

Now, at first jump, I do not try to draw the fine distinctions in Trinitarian theology. (For those theologians, let me say I am well aware of the great and important distinctions between Trinitarianism and Unitarianism. I am aware of the dangers of terms like "manifestations." I know the difference between Persons and theophanies.) For now, I will settle for drawing the Mormon's attention to the omnipotence, omniscience, and omnipresence of God. I want him to see that God is much bigger than Mormon theology allows Him to be. I want Mormons simply to admit that it is possible for Him to be in more than one place visible in more than one way—simultaneously.

The key phrase in this discussion is, "Once your God is big enough, you won't have any problems with the Trinity."

5. Didn't Jesus Tell Us We Are to "Be Perfect, Even as Our Father in Heaven is Perfect"?

This is an argument leading to the Mormon concept that with perfection we will become gods. When I am asked about Jesus' command to perfection, I say:

"Yes, He sure did command us to be perfect. And I'm all for it. I want to be perfect, just as my Father in heaven is perfect. And I expect to be perfect in heaven.

"Of course, I will be a perfect *human*. I won't be omnipotent, or omniscient, or omnipresent—because I am not God. I'm a man—a *creature*, that is, a created being.

"I will be perfect, just as He is perfect. He's the perfect God. I will be a perfect human."

6. Don't We Need a Prophet Today?

Mormonism tells us we need a Prophet today to clear up confusion among the denominations, to which I answer:

"No, we don't need a prophet to clear up confusion because, *really, there isn't much confusion.* I could be happy as a Baptist or a Lutheran or a Methodist or an Episcopalian. I go to church with friends who affiliate with denominations other than my own, and I have a blast."

Early churches didn't have a lesson manual from Jerusalem. The apostles in Jerusalem were reluctant to tell the Church much of *anything*, saying the individual churches had Scripture and the guidance of the Holy Spirit. They could figure out what the will of God was for the local church (Acts 15:5–29).

"That's the way it is today," I say to my Mormon contact. "In God there is plenty of room for different expressions in nonessential doctrinal areas. Some Christians like to praise and worship with vigor and volume. Some like to contemplate the glory of God in solemnity. Why not? God doesn't want robots; He wants sons.

"There is, of course, a biblical minimum that all churches must confess in order to fit into the larger Christian Church. These doctrines are related to the nature of God, the nature of man, the effect of and cure for sin. Beyond that, the Bible allows great liberty. In fact, Paul said, 'It is for freedom that Christ has set us free' (Galatians 5:1).

"When we were slaves to Satan, we jumped when he pulled the strings. God doesn't want us to trade that slavery in for another form of bondage. He wants to liberate us and set us free to be all we can be, within biblical bounds.

"I won't rule out the possibility that God will speak prophetically through someone today. I think that happens, for example, in preaching and counseling. But, any prophet must be accountable to Scripture. God doesn't contradict Himself. The Bible makes it clear that a prophet who speaks contrary to Scripture, is no prophet (Deuteronomy 18:21–22).

"Nowhere in Scripture do we see the Mormon concept of a prophet as the head of a church organization. This concept is purely a Mormon invention. In Scripture, ordinary people could be prophets if they prophesied. Even those prophets recognized in the Old Testament by the entire church were often contemporaries of each other. Many of the four major prophets and twelve minor prophets (whose names entitle sixteen of the last books of the Old Testament) were prophesying as men living at the same time."

7. You Shouldn't Challenge Our "Good Works"; Don't You Know That Faith Without Works is Dead?

"I sure do. If a person says he has faith in Christ, and yet exhibits no fruit of that faith, I have reason to doubt the validity of his faith. That's because valid faith always produces fruit. But, on the other hand, fruit doesn't produce faith. No amount of good works will make people Christians.

"Lots of agnostics live wonderful 'Christian' lives, but they don't believe in Christ. Their 'fruit' doesn't make them Christians, nor, the Bible teaches, does it save them. Good works can't save anybody.

"Likewise, Muslims are very 'religious.' They don't drink, they pray five times a day, they live with more legalistic taboos than Mormons, but they certainly cannot be called Christians, and they certainly are not saved.

"And nobody lives better lives than Oriental Americans. Their families are in order, the crime rate in Chinatown is a fraction of the rate in the rest of the country, people there are hard-working, and their children are respectful. But a person isn't a Christian because he is good; however he does become better when he commits his life to Christ."

If you have a Bible during this encounter, read the following passage to your Mormon friend.

> There is no one righteous, not even one. . . . Therefore, no one will be declared righteous in [God's] sight by observing the law. . . . But now a righteousness from God, apart from law, has been made known. . . . This righteousness from God comes through faith in Jesus Christ to all who believe. There is no difference, for all have sinned and fall short of the glory of God, and are justified freely by his grace through the redemption that came by Christ Jesus. God presented him as a sacrifice of atonement . . . [to justify] the man who has faith in Jesus. . . . For we maintain that a man is justified by faith apart from observing the law (Romans 3:10, 20–28).

Paul says that Abraham was not justified by works, but rather that he believed God, and God counted his faith as righteousness (Romans 4:3). He further says, if a man works, his wages are not a gift, but an obligation (Romans 4:4).

> However, to the man who does not work but trusts God who justifies the wicked, his faith is credited as righteousness (Romans 4:5).

8. Why Do You Oppose Our Idea of Becoming Gods? The Bible Says, "There are Gods Many and Lords Many."

"The Bible does *not* say that! It says exactly the opposite." (Be tough on nonsense like this.)

The reference is 1 Corinthians 8:5. But the problem is that Mormonism has taken the text out of context so that it appears to mean exactly the opposite of what it says.

Say to the Latter-day Saint: "If you'll read the verse right before it and right after it, you'll see that Paul is talking about demon-gods. The issue he is addressing is whether or not Christians should eat food sacrificed to demons (idols) in the pagan marketplace. He says that while there are so-called 'gods,' Christians know there is only one God. Therefore, the meat has not been hurt because it hung in a pagan temple."

This is a wonderful place to open your Bible and go through the passage a verse at a time, letting the Mormon read it aloud.

9. You Say the Book of Mormon Was Not Written by God, but How Could a Fifteen-Year-Old Boy Write the Book of Mormon?

The idea expressed here is that the Book of Mormon is too long, complex, and intricate for "a young, uneducated boy" (Joseph Smith) to have made up. Several assumptions are made in this question. Here are two real considerations:

First, Joseph was twenty-five, *not fifteen* when he published (as "author" and "proprietor," according to the title page of the first edition) the Book of Mormon.

Second, the Book of Mormon heavily plagiarized the content of other works already in print and available in Joseph's area, including *View of the Hebrews,* by Ethan Smith, and another work by Solomon Spalding, *Manuscript Found!*

(The Mormon Church historically has attempted to debunk the "Spalding Theory" but new evidence underscores Spalding as a likely source. See Appendix C.)

Could Joseph Smith in an entirely human way have "written" the Book of Mormon? Well, one of the most respected Mormon apologists of all time, Brigham H. Roberts, concluded he *did*. (See Appendix B.)

This chapter has given you practice in responding to questions Mormons may ask you. In the next section I am going to provide some background information to help you initiate profitable discussions with Mormons.

Part 3

Advanced Encounters

Chapter Twelve

Some Topics You Should Understand

"During my first semester at college, the very liberal theology of the school changed my spiritual views. I lost touch with my Savior and entered a very dark period of my life. During second semester, Mormon missionaries spoke to my sociology class. I was intrigued and called them up and was baptized into the Mormon Church against the wishes of my parents and many of my friends.

"The reason I'm writing is [to say that] ... I'm back in touch with my Savior, Jesus Christ! I'm not saying it has been easy, far from it. I'm also not saying it's complete since the local missionaries and Church members have been calling daily for me to reconsider...."

Becky

My plan in this chapter is to give you some background into some of the doctrinal stands of Mormonism that range from abominable to silly. If you bring these topics up, you will be in a good position to break through petrified Mormon mindsets. You will get a taste of areas like:

—The Virgin Birth
—Blood Atonement
—Conflicting Prophecies

Then I will touch on several other subjects that you can begin to study on your own.

The Virgin Birth—Mormon Style

In Chapter Six I recounted the conversation I had with my mother-in-law about the Virgin Birth. The discussion centered on Mormon doctrine regarding the birth of Jesus. Audrey claimed that she believed (and that the Mormon Church *taught*) that Jesus was conceived by the Holy Ghost.

Knowing that Mormonism does *not* teach that, I told her that while *she* apparently believed good, sound Bible doctrine, the Mormon *Church* didn't. Mormon doctrine teaches that God the Father had sexual relations with Mary in order to procreate Christ.

Audrey objected vigorously. She said that doctrine was repugnant to her and her Church taught no such thing. She correctly stated that the Bible explicitly taught that "the Holy Ghost came upon Mary," at conception.

I persistently led her into an argument on the subject. *I let her establish, by her own arguments, that such a doctrine is, indeed, repugnant.* I wanted her to develop her innate sense of right and wrong, which stood in stark opposition with this doctrine of the Mormon Church.

Since the subject—the Virgin Birth—already was *isolated,* I proceeded to *qualify.* I didn't ask for much: only that she admit that her Church taught a doctrine contrary to the Bible. She said that *if* the Church taught the doctrine (and she was sure it *didn't*), then it taught an unbiblical doctrine. She conceded that if I could produce statements from five General Authorities of Mormonism saying Jesus was conceived by natural relations, then her Church actually did teach that wrong concept.

Now, by producing those statements, I created a real dilemma for her. Seeing Mormon doctrine in strong juxtaposition with Bible doctrine, she had serious reason to doubt the Mormon claims of divine revelation. Here is the documentation I provided Audrey:

First, Brigham Young said:

When the Virgin Mary conceived the child Jesus, the Father had begotten him in his own likeness. He was not begotten by the Holy Ghost.... Remember from this time forth, and for ever, that Jesus Christ was not begotten by the Holy Ghost.... In fact ... if the Son was begotten by the Holy Ghost, it would be very dangerous to baptize and confirm females, and give the Holy Ghost to them, lest he should beget children to be palmed upon the Elders by the people, bringing the Elders into great difficulties.[1]

The birth of the Savior was as natural as are the births of our children; it was the result of natural action ... [Jesus] ... was begotten of his Father, as we were of our fathers.[2]

Young also said that the Father did it Himself, "instead of letting any other man do it."[3]

Second, Orson Pratt said the Father and Mary *must* have been married if God overshadowed her:

The Father and Mother of Jesus, according to the flesh, must have been associated together in the capacity of Husband and Wife; hence the Virgin Mary must have been, for the time being, the lawful wife of God the Father; we use the term lawful Wife because it would have been blasphemous in the highest degree to say that He overshadowed her or begat the Saviour unlawfully.[4]

Third, Heber C. Kimball said there was *nothing supernatural* about the birth of Jesus:

I will say that I was naturally begotten; so was my father and also my Saviour, Jesus Christ. According to the Scriptures, he is the first begotten of his father in the flesh and there was nothing unnatural about it.[5]

1. *Journal of Discourses*, Vol. 1, pp. 50–51.
2. *Journal of Discourses*, Vol. 8, p. 115.
3. *Journal of Discourses*, Vol. 4, p. 218.
4. Pratt, p. 158.
5. *Journal of Discourses*, Vol. 8, p. 211.

Fourth, Bruce McConkie said:

> [Christ] was born in the same personal, real, and literal sense as any mortal son is born to a mortal father. There is nothing figurative about his paternity; he was ... conceived and born in the normal and natural course of events.[6]

Fifth, Joseph Fielding Smith said:

> Christ was ... not born without the aid of man and that man was God.[7]

The Mormon Doctrine of Blood Atonement

Blood atonement in Mormon doctrine says it is sometimes necessary to "shed a man's blood to save his soul." The idea is that he can commit sins that are so grievous that *he can only go to heaven if his own* blood is shed, that is, if he is killed. This grisly doctrine postulates the idea that somehow in killing him there is expiation for his sins. Blood Atonement was not only preached in Utah, it was also practiced.

This doctrine, which completely contradicts the atoning work of the shed blood of Christ, was birthed in a vision of Joseph Smith's in which he said he was visited by the apostle Peter who told him that he (Peter) had killed Judas—that he had *hung him* for betraying Christ.[8]

Mormon President Heber C. Kimball also preached the murder of Judas. He said, "They kicked him until his bowels came out." And he warned the Elders to be careful not to

---

6. McConkie, p. 742.
7. Joseph Fielding Smith, *Doctrines of Salvation,* Bookcraft Publishers, Salt Lake City, Vol. 1, p. 18.
8. *Reed Peck Manuscript,* Reprinted by Utah Lighthouse Ministry, Salt Lake City, p. 13.

"forfeit their covenants," because the day was at hand when they would be destroyed "as Judas was."[9]

Brigham Young, as usual, carried the doctrine to its logical ultimate conclusion. He said if he found a brother in bed with his wife he would:

> ... Put a javelin through both of them, [and be] justified, and they would atone for their sins, and be received into the kingdom of God. ... I would do it with clean hands. ... There is not a man or woman, who violates the covenants made with their God, that will not be required to pay the debt. *The blood of Christ will never wipe that out, your own blood must atone for it.*[10]

And Brother Brigham was as good as his word. He ordered people ritually slain "to atone for their sins."

Brigham Young frequently made public reference to a Mormon organization known as the "Destroying Angels," or "Danites," in threatening language. "If men come here and do not behave themselves, they will ... find the Danites ... biting their heels."

Men like John D. Lee and Bill Hickman and Porter Rockwell carried out dozens of official Brigham-ordered murders. These stories are recounted in autobiographies like *The Confessions of John D. Lee* and *Brigham's Destroying Angel* by Hickman. John D. Lee was executed for his part in the Mountain Meadows Massacre—the massacre of a wagon train of Missouri pioneers. Lee, who testified that he was only carrying out Brigham's orders, was shot as he sat on the edge of his coffin.

John D. Lee told of the Mormon-ordered execution of Rosmos Anderson for adultery. Anderson was taken from his home at midnight, led to a grave site near Cedar City and

9. *Journal of Discourses*, Vol. 6, pp. 125–126.
10. *Journal of Discourses*, Vol. 3, p. 247.

held while his throat was slit and the blood ran into the grave. The executioner then dressed him in a new suit, buried him, and returned his bloody clothing to his wife.[11]

So widespread was the knowledge of the doctrine of Blood Atonement that the Utah capital punishment law was written to include a form of death that would shed blood. At one time, a man condemned to death could even choose to have his throat slit. Throat-slitting seemed to be the coup of choice in early Utah. *Even to this day all participants in Mormon temple ceremonies place their right thumbs under their left ears and draw the thumb quickly across the throat to the right ear to "symbolize the penalty" for revealing the temple ceremony.* Participants are agreeing to their own executions if they reveal the secret temple oaths.

Today fallout from Blood Atonement continues to settle in the red Utah dust. Recently Ron Lafferty, a former Mormon leader in Utah, was convicted of ritually slitting the throat of his sister-in-law, Brenda, and her eighteen-month-old daughter. Both Brenda and her baby were ritually slain in obedience to a "revelation" that said, in part:

> Thus sayeth the Lord unto my servants the prophets. It is my will and commandment that ye remove the following individuals in order that my work might go forward, for they have truly become obstacles in my path and I will not allow my work to be stopped.
>
> First thy brother's wife, Brenda, and her baby, then Chole Low, and then Richard Stowe. And it is my will that they be removed in rapid succession and that an example be made of them in order that others might see the fate of those who fight against the true saints of God.

The Lafferty brothers claimed that the slayings were not crimes but rather "the fulfillment of a revelation from God."

11.   John D. Lee, *Confessions of John D. Lee,* Bryan, Brand & Company, St. Louis, 1877, pp. 282–283.

When he was found guilty, Lafferty's lawyer said his client chose the firing squad "because of blood atonement."[12]

In another grotesque "test of faith" a student at Utah State University plunged a huge butcher knife (purchased for the occasion by his wife) into the breast of his infant son, killing him. Rodney Lundberg did three years in a mental hospital and is now free.[13]

The Conflicting and False Prophecies of Mormondom

The Mormon Church is supposedly the "Church of the Restoration." Joseph Smith was to restore the "plain and precious truths which had been lost." The agent of the restoration is revelation.

The facts, however, don't match the claim. Mormonism confuses more than it clears up. Mormonism is replete with conflicting prophesies like these:

Polygamy: **Book of Mormon** Behold, David and Solomon truly had many wives and concubines, which thing *was abominable before me*, saith the Lord (Jacob 2:24).	**Polygamy:** **Joseph Smith** I, the Lord, *justified* ... David and Solomon ... as touching the principle and doctrine of their having many wives and concubines.[14]
God Changeable: **Wilford Woodruff** God himself is increasing and progressing in knowl-	**God Unchangeable:** **Joseph Fielding Smith** The doctrine "God increases in knowledge as

12. *Idaho Falls Post Register,* "Lafferty Decides on Firing Squad," May 8, 1986.
13. From Associated Press wire copy in author's possession, 5/9/85.
14. *Doctrine and Covenants,* Sec. 132, vs. 1.

edge, power and dominion, and will do so worlds without end.[15]

One God:
Book of Mormon
And Zeezrom said unto him: ... is there more than one God? And he [Amulek] answered, No (Alma 11:26–29).

Never Give Up Polygamy:
Brigham Young
Do you think we shall ever be admitted as a State into the Union without denying the principal of polygamy? If we are not admitted until then, we shall never be admitted. These things are just as the Lord will.[18]

Adam—Not Earth Dust:
Brigham Young
Adam was made from the dust of *an* earth, *but not the dust of this earth.*[20]

time goes on" ... is very dangerous. I don't know where the Lord has ever declared such a thing.[16]

Many Gods:
Brigham Young
How many Gods there are, I do not know. But there never was a time when there were not Gods.[17]

Manifesto:
Wilford Woodruff
I hereby declare my intention to submit to [the polygamy laws], and to use my influence with the members of the Church ... to have them do likewise.[19]

Adam—Earth Dust:
Joseph Fielding Smith
Adam's body was created from the dust of the ground, that is, from the dust of *this ground, this earth.*[21]

15. *Journal of Discourses*, Vol. 6, p. 120.
16. Smith, *Doctrines of Salvation*, Vol. 1, pp. 7–8.
17. *Journal of Discourses*, Vol. 7, p. 333.
18. *Journal of Discourses*, Vol. 11, p. 269.
19. *Manifesto*, Sept. 24, 1890; *Doctrine and Covenants* official declaration #1.
20. *Journal of Discourses*, Vol 3, p. 319.
21. Smith, *Doctrines of Salvation*, Vol. 1, p. 90.

Adam-God:
Spencer W. Kimball
We denounce [the Adam-God Theory] and hope that everyone will be cautioned against this and other kinds of *false doctrine*.[22]

Adam-God:
Brigham Young
How much unbelief exists ... in regard to one particular doctrine ... which God revealed to me—namely that Adam is our father and God.[23]

No Paid Ministry

The Mormon Church makes much of the fact that it has no paid ministry. It also denigrates, in the temple ceremony, ministers who "preach for pay." Nevertheless, every General Authority receives remuneration for his services. In most instances, salaries are paid. In addition, General Authorities invariably sit on the boards of directors of Church-owned corporations like U & I Sugar and Beneficial Life Insurance. The First Presidency and Apostles make tens of thousands of dollars from the Church or Church-owned companies.[24]

The Book of Abraham

Joseph Smith said he translated the Book of Abraham from Egyptian papyri he bought from a traveling exhibition. He "translated" it and presented it to his Church as Scripture. To this day it is part of the *Pearl of Great Price.*

22. *Deseret News,* Oct. 9, 1976.
23. *Deseret News,* June 18, 1873.
24. Tanner, *Mormonism—Shadow or Reality?*, pp. 516, 527; John Heinerman and Anson Shupe, *The Mormon Corporate Empire,* Beacon Press, Boston, 1985; Robert Gottlieb and Peter Wiley, *America's Saints,* G.P. Putnam's Sons, New York, 1984.

What he thought was a record of Abraham in Egypt is really an Egyptian funeral text. It has since been translated by several Egyptologists who are in total agreement on that.[25]

Failed and False Prophecies and Revelations

The study of false, failed, and just plain inane prophecies is a field itself. In *Beyond Mormonism* I listed these:

—Joseph Smith said that men live on the moon, are tall, about six feet, dress like Quakers, and live to be 1,000 years old.[26]

—Brigham Young said men inhabit the sun.[27]

—Joseph prophesied that Jesus would return by 1891.[28]

—Brigham said the Civil War would not free the slaves.[29]

—Brigham said the earth was alive.[30]

—Orson Pratt said that before men and women are born on earth as babies, their spirits are adult-sized in heaven. When they are born, their spirits are compressed, which causes a loss of memory.[31]

—Orson also said vegetables have spirits, are the offspring of male and female vegetable spirits, and are capable of being happy.[32]

As you speak with Mormons these subjects probably won't come up unless you bring them up. They are not listed here so that Mormons may be wounded or ridiculed, but so

25. Tanner, *Mormonism—Shadow or Reality*, "The Fall of the Book of Abraham," pp. 294–369.
26. *The Young Woman's Journal*, Vol. 3, p. 263.
27. *Journal of Discourses*, Vol. 13, p. 271.
28. *History of the Church*, Vol. 2, p. 182.
29. *Journal of Discourses*, Vol. 10, p. 250.
30. *Journal of Discourses*, Vol. 6, p. 36.
31. *Journal of Discourses*, Vol. 16, pp. 333–334.
32. Pratt, pp. 33–34.

that you will have information to use to snake them out of complacency. I pray that you will use wisdom, compassion, yet unfailing determination to rescue Mormons from the insanity of Mormonism.

Chapter Thirteen

The Mormon Family

"My husband, Ralph, and I have been members of the LDS Church since July 1979. We were shocked at your book and at the same time relieved. We were taking classes to prepare us and our two daughters to go to the temple. We have asked members of our ward many times what we would have to do once we were in the temple. And the answer has always been, 'When it's time for you to know, you will be told.' Our questions have never been answered.

"We need to know more—we are at a complete loss. And I'm really afraid."

Alexandria

You never really encounter Latter-day Saints alone. Hovering over every conversation is a family network contradicting your every statement, clouding every issue, and confounding reason.

The young Mormon man with whom you are talking once sat in a Primary circle singing, "I Hope They Call Me on a Mission." His dad promised to send him to college and buy him a new car—*after* he returned from his mission. "I would have shamed my family terribly," a tough ex-cop told me, "if I had not served a two-year mission. I had no choice."

Women drag their kids to the pharmacy to get their monthly Valium prescription filled because they cannot bring themselves to take birth control pills. They've been carefully taught that "spirit children" in heaven are patiently waiting to be "born under the covenant" (that is, to come to earth and "take on bodies" in a good Mormon home).

In Utah, which is two-thirds Mormon, family life is advertised in TV and radio spots as slices from "Father Knows Best." But in reality, social scientists are pessimistic about the quality of Utah family life. (See statistical footnotes in Chapter Two.)

Bringing Latter-day Saints to Christ almost always precipitates a family crisis as loved ones react with fear and anger. Sometimes family problems reach gigantic proportions. Christians often are unprepared for the furor that follows the conversion of a Latter-day Saint. If you are to evangelize Mormons, you need to be prepared for the heartbreak of watching the new Christian experience rejection and ostracism.

Mormonism is a closed system. Many Mormons have no social life outside their Church. They may go off to Gentile jobs each morning, but when they come home, it is to a Mormon family and Mormon Church activities.

For Mormons, salvation is a family affair. Eternal marriage, on the one hand, and genealogy, on the other, attempt to extend the family relationship into eternity. That means that when somebody leaves the Church, he endangers the salvation of other family members. Many people have told me stories like this: A young man was born again. His Mormon bishop called him in and told him that unless he changed his mind, it would be necessary for his wife "to find someone else to take her to the Celestial Kingdom." When a Mormon leaves the Church, especially when a *man* leaves the Church, the marriage is in peril.

Therefore, we must move with utmost sensitivity as we deal with Mormon families. We must attempt to preserve the marriage at all costs except the loss of the eternal soul. I tell people who come to Christ to be very careful and patient with their Latter-day Saint spouses. Let them come at their own speed. Do nothing to rush them.

In my own case, when I was born again, I told my wife that we would raise our children as Mormons. And I refrained from being water baptized as a Christian for two years. (God arranged it so that by the time I *was* baptized, my wife was ready to join me.)

The Bible says the spouse will be won by the godly behavior, not by witnessing and argument. A life lived flat out for Christ with tenderness and sensitivity to the feelings of the unsaved spouse will do more than Scripture-quoting and arguing. When I told my wife that we could raise our children as Mormons, I was honoring the vow I made to her at marriage. I knew God would protect my children until my wife was saved. And as a matter of fact, my eight-year-old daughter made a public profession of Christ the same night my wife did.

I was very fortunate. Not every man who leaves Mormonism for Christ keeps his family. And we must be prepared to press our witness to the limit in spite of the dangers involved. It's a great responsibility and we'd better be sure our hearts and motives are pure as we interfere in the lives of others.

Women in Mormonism stand in a unique position: Mormonism is unashamedly patriarchal. Women do not hold the priesthood. They are dependent upon their husbands to enter the highest levels of the Celestial Kingdom. Mormonism has adopted, practiced, and championed polygamy, something no other sub-culture in the Western civilized world has done.

Personally, I think it is impossible to understand Mormon family structure without understanding the horrors of polygamy. Although the Utah Mormon Church no longer practices polygamy (as Mormon fundamentalists in Mormondom do openly), it is still a doctrine of the Church. Mormons expect to practice polygamy in heaven. As a matter of fact, I would not be surprised to see the Utah Church again sanction the practice in our day. Why not? If fornication, trial marriages, and adultery are no longer crimes in our culture, if we are not going to send men to jail for living with more than one woman—out of wedlock—how are we going to be able to justify convicting men for doing so within the bounds of wedlock? And if the public accepts polygamy as legal, the Mormon Church is free to reinstitute the practice at will.

Polygamy not only illustrates the repression of women in Mormon society, it epitomizes the Church's powerful system of mind control. When you understand Mormon mind control, you are beginning to comprehend the essence of Mormonism.

Men as well as women were victims of this practice. By circumventing the New Testament standard, men were placed in a position of power that brought out the worst in them.

But, of course, it was the women who bore the pain and degradation of polygamy.

The History of Mormon Polygamy

The Book of Mormon condemns polygamy in very strong terms (Jacob 2:23–27), but Mormons were accused of polygamy from the earliest days of Mormonism. Their Church officially denied the charge, declaring that "one man should have one wife...." (Section 104 of the first edition of the *Doctrine and Covenants* declared that the Church believed polygamy to be a crime.)

The public declaration, however, was a cover-up for Joseph Smith's real feelings. One of his close friends testified that he was practicing polygamy as early as 1835 when the Church was in Kirtland, Ohio.[1] The first woman the already-married Joseph Smith took to be his wife was Fannie

1. Tanner, *Mormonism—Shadow or Reality,* p. 203–204.

Alger a "comely young girl" who lived with the Smiths in Kirtland. Apostle John Widtsoe said Fannie lived many years after the Prophet's death and never denied her relationship with him.[2]

When Joseph finally came out of the closet, he brought polygamy as a commandment of the Lord. He said he received the revelation on plural marriage on July 12, 1843 (just less than a year before his death). Anticipating resistance (and his wife Emma's reaction), Joseph couched the prophecy in strong language:

> If ye abide not that covenant, then are ye damned. . . . And let my handmaiden, Emma Smith, receive all those that have been given unto my servant Joseph. . . . But if she will not abide this commandment she shall be destroyed.[3]

Emma, to say the least, was not pleased with the revelation. Joseph wrote it out and his brother, Hyrum, took it to Emma to read. Hyrum returned to tell Joseph he had "never received a more severe talking to in his life." In fact, Emma took the revelation from Joseph and destroyed it.[4]

Amazingly, although Joseph was practicing polygamy from 1835 on, and while the official revelation on the subject came in 1843, and while the practice was widespread in Utah from 1847, the Church continued to publish the 1835 revelation against polygamy until 1876.

The Woe of Polygamy

Mormon polygamy was born, I believe, in the lust of Joseph Smith. Again, Brigham Young carried it to the ultimate conclusion with at least twenty-seven wives.

2. Tanner, *Mormonism—Shadow or Reality*, p. 203.
3. *Doctrine and Covenants*, Sec. 132, vs. 4, 52, 54.
4. *History of the Church*, Introduction to Vol. 5, p. XXXII.

But polygamy was a spiritual regression. Although God tolerated both divorce and polygamy in the Old Testament, the clear teaching of the Bible is the Genesis 2:23–24 idea that man and woman come together in a divinely ordained "two." Jesus reiterates that in Matthew 19:3–9 and Mark 10:1–12.

Likewise, Paul calls the Church to monogamy in 1 Timothy 3:2. In eloquent terms he sets forth the high biblical calling of mutual submission in the monogamous marriage relationship in Ephesians 5:23–33.

Brigham Young said women ought simply to "be happy to have a man from the Lord! . . . Sisters . . . what is your duty? It is for you to bear children." Women shouldn't torment themselves with whether or not their husbands loved them, Brigham said, but should just shout "Hallelujah!" that they have a man.[5]

Even faithful Mormon polygamists understood the heartbreak of polygamy. One wrote, "Plural marriage .. . is calculated in its nature to severely try the women, even to nearly tear their heart strings out of them."[6]

The manipulation Joseph Smith exercised through polygamy was illustrated when he demanded to have Vilate, the wife of Heber C. Kimball. Kimball sweated and prayed for three days before bringing her to Joseph, who then told him it was really just "a test of his loyalty." A few days later, however, Joseph accepted Kimball's eldest daughter, Helen Mar—in "half-ripe bud of womanhood." (Many believed Kimball had struck a deal with Joseph, trading Helen Mar for Vilate.)

Brigham Young had little patience with his wives who complained about the institution of polygamy:

You must fulfill the law of God in every respect, and round up your shoulders to walk up to the mark without

5. *Journal of Discourses,* Vol. 9, p. 37.
6. Tanner, *Mormonism—Shadow or Reality,* p. 209.

any grunting....There is no cessation to the everlasting whining of many of the women in this territory.... I will not hear any more of this whining.[7]

In an attempt to justify polygamy, Mormon Church leaders even taught that *Jesus was a polygamist!* "If he was never married," apostle Orson Hyde said, "his intimacy with Mary and Martha, and the other Mary ... must have been highly unbecoming and improper to say the least."[8]

Mormondom has never recovered from polygamy. The Church still attempts to force women into roles as subordinate baby factories. And every female Latter-day Saint must reconcile herself to the belief of polygamy in heaven.

The Woman in Modern Mormonism

What is it like to be a modern Mormon woman? And how can we reach into the Mormon family with the Gospel of Christ? Is there life for the post-Mormon woman?

Recently my wife, Margaretta, reflected on the unique position of the Mormon woman in a piece for our newsletter, "Through the Maze." This column so impressed His Majesty the King of Tonga, that he himself (a born-again and very evangelical Christian) translated it into Tonganese and reprinted it in a large-circulation Methodist newspaper. I reprint it here:

"I was born and raised as a Mormon in the land of Zion. My earliest memory is my desire to be married in the temple. I wanted to have my family sealed to me for time and all eternity, just as *I* was sealed to *my* family. This seemed like such a wonderful thing to me. I pitied the poor Gentiles who would only be with their families for this life.

"As I grew older, I acquired another motive for temple

7. *Journal of Discourses*, Vol. 4, pp. 55–57.
8. *Journal of Discourses*, Vol. 4, pp. 259–260.

marriage. My teacher in the Mutual Improvement Association had not married her husband in the temple. She often related to our Mutual class that since she had not married her husband in the temple, she would be a servant in the Celestial Kingdom. She would have to wait on tables and take care of the babies of those who had been more faithful. She would never be able to become a goddess to populate and rule worlds with her god-husband.

"I determined that I would never be a servant and wait on others; I would have a world of my own with my husband. I do not ever recall hearing that Jesus had said, 'If you want to be great in the Kingdom of God, you must be the servant of all.'

"I judged my Mutual teacher harshly. I considered her weak because she and her husband had not gotten themselves worthy to go through the temple.

"I promised myself I would never compromise on the issue of temple marriage. And I didn't! In 1966 Jim and I were married in the Idaho Falls temple. I was able to wear the holy garments and the way was now clear for me to make it to the highest degree of glory in the Celestial King dom. I would, of course, have to continue to keep myself worthy, but I really felt I had accomplished my goal.

"Looking back now over my thirty years of Mormonism and my ten years as a born-again Christian, I am able to compare two quite different lives. I am able to see the difference between being a Mormon woman and being a Christian woman.

"As a Mormon woman of unshakable faith and testimony, I was often called upon to believe things that were so unbelievable I was forced to simply put them out of my mind. For example, I was taught that in the last days, many men would be killed and my husband might be forced to take other women as his wives to keep them safe under the Covenant. I didn't like to think about that.

"I also knew that in the resurrection, my husband would

have to call me out of the grave, using a name given me in the temple. I wasn't sure I could trust Jim's memory! (A friend's husband did forget her name and had to go back to the temple to get it again.) I also worried that Jim might just decide not to call me out.

"When Jim left the Church, the Stake President warned him that if he didn't repent, I would be given to another man in the resurrection. I especially didn't like to think that my destiny could be changed by the whim of my husband or some other man, and that I had no say in the matter.

"After I became a Christian woman, I began to see that Jesus has a special plan for all women. I began to experience the joy in my destiny as a woman of God. I read in the Bible that: 'You are all sons of God through faith in Christ Jesus, for all of you who were baptized into Christ have clothed yourselves with Christ. There is neither Jew nor Greek, slave nor free, male nor female, for you are all one in Christ Jesus' (Galatians 3:26–28).

"This does not mean that there is no order in Christian living. Jesus has placed the husband at the head of the home. But this does not change my personal relationship with Jesus in any way. Jim is the head of our home. He is the spiritual covering for me and our children. I wouldn't have it any other way (most of the time!). But I am not under his thumb. I am a child of God through faith in Jesus Christ and I am an heir to all the promises of Abraham just the same as my husband is.

"It is exciting to know that Jesus considers me a child of God through faith, and an heir to *all* the promises of Abraham. I never have to worry that I will be kept out of any corner of the Kingdom of God by the whim of men. I will enter the same way any other child of God does—by faith in Jesus Christ as Lord and Savior, trusting in Him and Him alone. I cannot express the difference knowing these things has made in my life. I have literally experienced the promise of John 8:36: 'If the Son sets you free, you will be free indeed.' "

When we attempt to reach Mormons for Christ we are faced with entering their private worlds and speaking the word of truth to them. When we do that, families sometimes will be thrown into confusion.

I know there is no way to cut chains of bondage without the chance that the sword of liberation might also be a sword of division. Jesus Himself, the Great Liberator, said, "I did not come to bring peace, but a sword." He says anyone who loves family more than Him is not worthy of Him (Matthew 10:34–37).

A sword of division is in our hands. Frankly, I don't like it. I wish there were another way. In my finite wisdom, I question why God allows cults to exist. And why His Church is charged with the responsibility of confronting them.

God grant us the sensitivity and wisdom to cut the cords of bondage without harming the bound victims.

Chapter Fourteen

Encountering Mormon Salvation Theology

"I want to let you know that I'm finally free from Mormonism after more than a year of searching. Thank God.

"I feel totally and absolutely free from the bonds of Mormonism. My prayers were answered! I've finally come to know the Lord Jesus Christ, in a new and exciting way. For the first time I've felt the love of Christ and have been freed from the constant feelings of condemnation. I'm a sinner, but I'm forgiven! Something I as a Mormon never knew existed.

"I am now free to love Him instead of just fear Him."

Pam

A young "Jesus freak," a converted druggie, arrived in our town on a bus from the Midwest. He had spent two days arguing religion with a Jehovah's Witness. After a thousand miles the JW got off the bus. When it started up again, a little old lady, seated a row behind my friend leaned forward and said quietly, "Son, they can't understand the Bible until they're born again."

I think many evangelicals who encounter Mormons fail to understand this simple Pauline precept: "The message of the cross is foolishness to those who are perishing." This be-

comes especially apparent as we attempt to talk about salvation to Mormons. They use many of the same terms we
do, but they assign different meanings to them, so any discussion is loaded with semantic problems.

An example is the atonement, the sacrifice of Jesus on the
Cross to buy eternal life for all who accept that sacrifice for
their sins. To a Mormon the atoning work of Christ pays for
no personal sins. It merely buys physical resurrection for all
people—regardless of their faith.

"Hell" in Mormon theology is not the abode of all those
who fail to accept Christ. Virtually no one spends eternity in
hell—only "sons of perdition."

"Heaven" as a Mormon would understand it is reserved
for Mormons who fully obey the laws and ordinances of the
Mormon gospel. Mormon heaven actually includes three
heavens with the highest partitioned into three more levels.
The "exalted ones" in the highest level will become gods and
create and people their own worlds.

Because of these semantic problems I avoid discussing
salvation with a Mormon as long as I can.

I do so because I find a salvation discussion bogs down to
an exchange of salvos of Bible verses. For every verse you
show a Mormon emphasizing, for example, salvation as a
free gift from God, he will show you one emphasizing man's
responsibility in obedience. *Obedience is the one single most
important word in Mormon salvation theology; grace is the
one single most important word in Christian salvation theology.*

Another reason I postpone the discussion of salvation is
that for a Christian *a man is not saved by knowledge, or profession of doctrinal truth.* Many born-again Christians have
difficulty articulating their salvation—that doesn't mean
they aren't saved. Some could not write a coherent statement about the holy Trinity—but they're still born again.
Man is not saved by doctrine, but by relationship—

meeting Christ and accepting His atonement. Doctrinal clarification comes on the heels of relationship: It doesn't produce it.

Salvation is a heart change. When the rich young ruler came to Christ and asked, "What must I do to be saved?" Jesus didn't tell him. He said, rather, give up your riches, then you may begin your journey toward God (see Matthew 19:16–26). When Nicodemus came to Jesus to have a religious conversation, Jesus said, in effect, "You need a radical spiritual change, not a doctrinal discussion" (see John 3:1–21).

I strongly recommend that early conversations with Mormons avoid arguing about whether or not the Mormon is saved, but rather focus on introducing him to the nature of God, the nature of revelation, and the Book of Mormon.

These discussions will be more likely to lead a Mormon to Christ. Discussing what Jesus or the Bible says about salvation presupposes he knows Jesus and the Bible. But in fact, he does not. He knows a *different* Jesus. He knows a *different* Bible. He is blinded and has received "a different Jesus, a different gospel, and a different spirit."

We must first bring him to see the *real* God. Then show him the way God *really* speaks (through Scripture). Then show him the *real* Scripture. Then and only then, I believe, are you prepared to talk about how one is saved.

Bringing up salvation too early in the conversation may unduly discourage your Latter-day Saint friend. Telling him he is not a Christian may anger him and you may lose him. *So ask him to explain Mormon polytheism to you instead.* If you can get him to see that polytheism is unbiblical, you are well on your way to destroying the religious barriers *that keep him from salvation.* As long as the Mormon is clutching the idols of Mormonism—plurality of gods, Joseph Smith, the Book of Mormon, the Mormon social institution—he does not feel a *need* for salvation.

For these reasons, I call the discussion of salvation theol-

ogy an Advanced Encounter. I do not mean that the average
Christian cannot handle the discussion. With proper training, after the foundations have been laid, after the polish has
been knocked off the Mormon testimony, and after the Mormon comes to see that the Bible Jesus is not the Mormon
Jesus, there will come a time when he will be anxious to hear
the old, old story.

Understanding Mormon Salvation Theology

The essence of Mormon salvation is the belief that salvation is a "process." A process of obedience to "laws and ordinances." The Third Article of Faith says:

> We believe that through the Atonement of Christ, all
> mankind may be saved, by obedience to the laws and ordi-
> nances of the Gospel.

That means that only part of the process of salvation is
Jesus coming to die. The other part depends on man's continuing obedience.

The Fourth Article of Faith spells out what some of those
laws and ordinances are:

> We believe that the first principles and ordinances of the
> Gospel are (1) Faith in the Lord Jesus Christ; (2) Repen-
> tance; (3) Baptism by immersion for the remission of sins;
> (4) Laying on of hands for the gift of the Holy Ghost.

Note how many steps there are to salvation *added to* faith
in the Lord Jesus Christ. The atoning work of the Cross is
undone because it is only one step in a process. These steps,
we are told, put us on the path to "exaltation" in the Celestial Kingdom. That path is long and demanding. Mormon
Apostle Bruce R. McConkie, in his encyclopedic *Mormon
Doctrine,* a widely accepted work in the Mormon Church for
forty years, says:

An inheritance in [the celestial] kingdom is gained by
complete obedience to gospel or celestial law (Doctrine and
Covenants 88:16–32). By entering the gate of repentance
and baptism candidates find themselves on the strait and
narrow path leading to the celestial kingdom. By devotion
and faithfulness, by enduring to the end in righteousness
and obedience, it is then possible to merit a celestial re-
ward.[1]

I can vouch personally for how wearisome and frightening
is the burden of salvation through obedience. I remember
speaking with an elderly Mormon stake president, a man
"born under the covenant," who was one of the stalwarts of
my Ward in St. Anthony, Idaho.

"President," I said, "I've been a Mormon for ten years
and I don't feel much closer to the celestial kingdom than
when I first joined. I'm faithful in attendance and in tithing
and I'm morally clean. But I'm getting nowhere. How do I
know I'm going to make it to the celestial kingdom? I mean,
what about you? Are you going to the celestial kingdom?"

I'll never forget the moment that followed. I looked into
the wizened face of this old patriarch and in his dark eyes I
saw only fatigue, without a trace of hope.

"Jim," was his reply, "you know I can't answer that. No
one can. All I can say is that I'm trying."

Unconditional and Conditional Salvation

McConkie tells us of two salvations:

1. Unconditional or general salvation, that which comes
from grace alone without obedience to gospel law, consists
in the mere fact of being resurrected. . . . This is not the salvation which the saints [Mormons] seek. Those who gain
only this . . . salvation will . . . be damned; their eternal

1. McConkie, p. 116.

progression cut short. In eternity [they] will be ministering spirits to more worthy persons.

2. Conditional or individual salvation, that which comes by grace coupled with gospel obedience ... *follows* faith, repentance, baptism, receipt of the Holy Ghost, and continued righteousness to the end of one's mortal probation.[2]

There are at least six different estates to which men will be assigned, based upon their conduct in this and the next life. These states are: perdition, the telestial kingdom, the terrestrial kingdom, and three degrees of the celestial kingdom.

Mormonism teaches that when men die they go to a "spirit world," divided into two sections, "spirit prison" and "paradise," to await assignment to one of the heavenly kingdoms. During this time, prior to the resurrection, those in spirit prison may be evangelized by Mormon spirits from paradise.

In the *Doctrine and Covenants* (Mormon scripture) is a report of Joseph Smith's vision of hell. Satan is called "Perdition," an angel who rebelled against God. Those who "know [God's] power, and have been made partakers thereof ... [and who] *deny the truth and defy my power* ... are *sons* of perdition" (Section 76, vs. 31–32).

These sons of perdition are doomed to the lake of fire in "outer darkness." Apparently ignoring the images of the "lake of fire" and "outer darkness" Joseph Smith wasn't too worried about the sufferings of the damned. He said, "Hell is by no means the place this world of fools supposes it to be, but on the contrary, it is quite an agreeable place."[3]

McConkie says these sons of perdition are:

Those in this life who gain a perfect knowledge of the divinity of the gospel cause, a knowledge that comes only by

2. McConkie, p. 116.
3. *The Nauvoo Expositor,* June 7, 1844.

revelation from the Holy Ghost, and who then link themselves with Lucifer and come out in open rebellion.[4]

Joseph Smith calls this "the sin against the Holy Ghost."[5]
It is interesting to note that Section 76 says these are the

> . . . only ones on whom the second death shall have any
> power . . . the only ones who shall not be redeemed in due
> time of the Lord, after the sufferings of his wrath.[6]

Except for these sons of perdition, *"all the rest"* shall be
saved!

We have in Mormonism, then, a theology known as Universal Salvation, in which mankind is universally saved.
Mormonism's Universal Salvation is wrapped up in a complex theology in which the saved are relegated to five levels
of "glory," depending upon their works. (Oddly, although it
is clearly Universalist, the Book of Mormon soundly condemns Universalism.)

Not only do we find Universalism in Mormonism, but we
find a concept akin to purgatory. Some, "in due time," will
even come out of perdition. McConkie says that those who
will be assigned to the telestial kingdom will have first "suffered the wrath of God in hell until the last resurrection."
However, ultimately it is their destiny to "inherit telestial
glory."[7]

The Three Kingdoms of Heaven

"It [is] self-evident," Joseph Smith said, "that if God
rewarded every one according to the deeds done in the body,

4. McConkie, p. 746.
5. Smith, *Teachings of the Prophet Joseph Smith*, p. 358.
6. *Doctrine and Covenants*, Sec. 76, vs. 37–38.
7. McConkie, p. 640.

the term Heaven ... must include more kingdoms than one."[8] Here is how these kingdoms are described:

Celestial Kingdom. Section 76, as we have seen, begins with the sons of perdition. Then it describes those who inhabit the celestial kingdom. They are those who: (1) believe in Christ; (2) are properly baptized and confirmed by someone holding the appropriate priesthood authority; and (3) are cleansed from sin by keeping the commandments.[9]
These people are:

Priests and Kings. . . .They are gods. . . .These shall dwell in the presence of God and his Christ . . . these are they whose bodies are celestial.[10]

While he does not specify the exact catalog of celestial law, McConkie speaks of the "law of consecration" and "making one's calling and election sure" by *"undeviating and perfect devotion to the cause of righteousness."*[11]
This undeviating obedience is required even *after* one reaches the celestial kingdom, for not all will go on to the very highest levels of exaltation. Those who miss the mark in the celestial kingdom will be ministering servants to

Minister for those who are worthy of a far more, and an exceeding, and an eternal weight of glory.[12]

Terrestrial Kingdom. The terrestrial kingdom will be the domain of "honorable men of the earth" who either did not hear the Mormon gospel or who rejected it on the earth, but

8. *Doctrine and Covenants,* Sec. 76, Heading.
9. *Doctrine and Covenants,* Sec. 76, vs. 51–53.
10. *Doctrine and Covenants,* Sec. 76, vs. 56–70.
11. McConkie, pp. 116–118.
12. *Doctrine and Covenants,* Sec. 132, vs. 16–17; see also McConkie, p. 670.

received it in the spirit world before the resurrection. This
also will be the domain of lukewarm Mormons.[13]

Those who inhabit the terrestrial kingdom "receive the
Presence of the Son, but not the Father," and never get to
marry and continue in exaltation.

Telestial Kingdom. At the end of the millennium, the second resurrection takes place. All those who are not assigned
to outer darkness inherit the telestial kingdom. Most people
who ever live on the earth go to this kingdom, McConkie
says. This kingdom is for endless hosts who have been carnal, sensual and devilish, liars and thieves, sorcerers and
adulterers, blasphemers and murderers. Those who are un-
clean and immoral, who are proud and rebellious, who walk
in paths of wickedness, who are carnal and sensual, who do
not maintain standards of decency, uprightness and integ-
rity.[14]

And yet, even so, this is not a bad place to live:

> The glory of the telestial ... surpasses all understand-
> ing.... [And the inhabitants of this kingdom are] judged
> according to their works ... [and each receives] his own
> dominion, in the mansions which are prepared ... [and they
> are] servants of the Most High; but where God and Christ
> dwell they cannot come.[15]

An Incredible Gulf

An incredible gulf separates Mormon salvation from that
of the Bible.

Evangelicals understand that salvation comes through the

---

13. McConkie, p. 784, see also *Doctrine and Covenants,* Sec. 76, vs.
    71–80.
14. See McConkie, p. 778, and *Doctrine and Covenants,* Sec. 76, vs.
    81–112.
15. *Doctrine and Covenants,* Sec. 76, vs. 89, 111–112.

merits of the shed blood of Christ. Man is hopelessly lost in sin, unable to raise himself from the mire of his fallen nature, "dead in transgressions and sins" (Ephesians 2:1). We gratefully acknowledge that we are saved by grace alone (see Ephesians 2:8–9).

But a Mormon not only has to earn his acceptability in God's sight, but he has to earn his way up a ladder that stretches into the infinities on the way to godhood:

> Jesus treads in the tracks of his Father and inherits what God did before.... When you climb up a ladder, you must begin at the bottom and ascend step by step ... you must begin at the first and go on until you learn all the principles of exaltation. But ... it is not all comprehended in this world; it will be a great work to learn our salvation and exaltation even beyond the grave.[16]

The Mormon is committed to this process. It "makes sense" to him. That is because the natural mind rebels at the suggestion that we are sinners, that we are bad—separated from God. The natural mind says, "We're not *too* bad and with a little fix-up, we'll be *really good*."

So, the most "natural" thing in the world is that we begin a program of self-improvement that culminates in our full acceptability to God.

Man's answer always is some ascetic program of self-improvement toward acceptability. Buddhism, for example, teaches the Four Noble Truths and the Eightfold Path to righteousness; the Unification Church teaches the concept of indemnity, that man becomes good by living in the shadow of the True Parents (Sun Myung Moon and his wife); Hinduism teaches the Law of Karma, that man is reincarnated until he is refined enough to become one with the Kosmic Mind.

16. Smith, *Teachings of the Prophet Joseph Smith*, p. 348.

Every religion on the face of the earth, outside of Bible Christianity, teaches salvation by some form of self-improvement or self-righteousness. Mormonism is not unique in that respect.

God's Justice

All these self-help doctrines, in the final analysis, fail to deal with sin! Sin goes unpunished.

But God is a God of justice. He fixes penalty for sin and it must be paid. Sin without punishment makes a mockery of law. A good act cannot cancel a bad one. You cannot hate your neighbor and make up for it by loving your children; you cannot steal ten dollars from me and cancel out your debt by giving ten dollars to charity. The problem is, you still hate your neighbor and I'm still out ten dollars.

Punishment is not simply for the sake of rehabilitation. It is also for the sake of justice. It was not enough that the Nazi war criminals saw the error of their ways; the Holocaust demanded *justice*. God has decreed that no amount of mercy will rob His justice. He will "not leave the guilty unpunished" (see Exodus 34:5–7).

So the problem is that man is a sinner deserving punishment and no amount of good works will pay for the sin he has already committed. He universally broke God's law and earns a sentence of death. Man always sins and God always demands justice. There is, however, a just solution to the problem of sin, which is found in the Bible concept of *substitution*.

Surely he took up our infirmities and carried our sorrows, yet we considered him stricken by God, smitten by him, and afflicted. But he was pierced for our transgressions, he was crushed for our iniquities; the punishment that brought us peace was upon him, and by his wounds we are healed. We all, like sheep, have gone astray, each of us has turned to his own way; and the Lord has laid on him the iniquity of us all (Isaiah 53:4-6).

No cultist is able to grasp the Christian concept that "without the shedding of blood there is no forgiveness" (Hebrews 9:22). All cults—and Mormonism is no exception—relegate the Atonement to a symbolic event in which Christ simply demonstrated infinite love. The concept that His blood was payment for our individual sins escapes them.

Mormonism has great trouble with the sacrifice of Jesus.

Brigham Young explicitly stated that Jesus was *"not* [crucified for] the actual individual transgressions of the people, but only for Original Sin."[17] A modern Mormon scholar, Keith Norman, says that Jesus never understood his death to be a vicarious atoning sacrifice." Norman says it was Paul who developed the concept that Jesus' death was "an expiatory, atoning sacrifice to redeem others." He did this, Norman says, "to convert Hellenistic Romans to whom such a concept would make sense."[18]

The Bible says "there is a way that seems right to a man, but the end thereof is destruction." Mormonism has taken such a path. Whenever I give a Mormon one of my books, I write on the flyleaf this reference in which Paul writes of his beloved Jewish brothers. I think the passage applies to my Mormon brothers and sisters:

> Brothers, my heart's desire and prayer to God for the Israelites is that they may be saved. For I can testify about them that they are zealous for God, but their zeal is not based on knowledge. Since they did not know the righteousness that comes from God and sought to establish their

17. *Journal of Discourses,* Vol. 13, p. 143.
18. *Sunstone,* "Toward a Mormon Christology," Vol. 10, No. 4, pp. 20–21.

own, they did not submit to God's righteousness. Christ is
the end of the law so that there may be righteousness for
everyone who believes (Romans 10:1-4).

My theory is that it is a waste of time to talk to Mormons
about salvation until they have come to doubt the ability of
Mormonism to save them.

They are blind to the Gospel; the idea of the Cross is foolishness to them.

Only when the Mormon sees that Mormonism is wrong
will his false god, which blinds him to the Gospel, lose some
of its authority over him. Only then will he begin to ask,
"What must I do to be saved?"

Part 4

Wisdom for Exiting Mormons

Chapter Fifteen

New Hope in Dealing with Mormonism

"I'm doing a lot better than when you last heard from me. It seems like every day gets a little easier. Were you really praying for me all this time? Prayer must really work!

"My husband and I are very happy now. He doesn't even bring up divorce anymore. In fact, he told me this morning he thinks our marriage has improved since I've become a Christian. I almost fell over when he said that!"

Robin

For thirteen weeks in the fall of 1982, John Aloysius Farrell, an investigative reporter for the *Denver Post*, traveled the state of Utah researching a six-part series that ran as "Utah: Inside the Church State." In spite of his journalistic effort at objectivity, it is clear that Farrell was shocked by what he found. "The Church State is different," he said. "Crossing its border is like riding along a wrinkle in time."

Farrell found Utah "strange, weird, dizzying," a land where "everything seems just a few degrees out of plumb." Values in Utah seemed different. "The cheerful, skeptical pluralism of the other 49 states does not apply."[1]

1. *The Denver Post*, Special Reprint, "Utah: Inside the Church State," p. 6.

Farrell came back from investigating the Church State in Utah to join the American Civil Liberties Union because what he saw convinced him he could not afford to take his liberty for granted. Shirley Pedler is the head of the ACLU in Utah. She was born in a Mormon home and she echoes Farrell's sentiments:

> People in power here . . . don't quite recognize a distinction between church and state. . . . Things as hideous as what the South was famous for do in fact go on here in Utah. . . . There is a veneer that everything is lovely. . . . But underneath it's different. Mean, mean things go on in this state.[2]

Christian leaders who serve in Mormondom understand the term "Zion Curtain"—an epithet that is all too accurate. I couldn't help but see Mormonism in Arakady Shevchenko's *Breaking with Moscow.* Shevchenko, the highest-ranking Russian diplomat ever to defect to the U.S., describes the flawed philosophy that forces some Russians to leave the Motherland:

> Beneath the multiplicity of reasons, there was one common denominator. At the bottom, it was the Soviet system that pushed its subjects to desperation, curtailing their freedoms or forcing them against their convictions.

Today life in Utah is changing because many Latter-day Saints have been pushed to desperation.

The winds of change are blowing in Mormonism. A great spiritual weariness goes with being an active Mormon. In the system you are on a treadmill with no hope of getting off, which helps explain why:

—Evangelical churches in Utah and other Mormon strong-

2. *The Denver Post,* Special Reprint, "Utah: Inside the Church State," pp. 7–8.

holds are splitting at the seams and going to two services.

—A Southern Baptist church in Vernal, Utah (which had been a mission church for forty years) suddenly went from 70 to 270 members in four months.

—Nearly one-half of my own congregation is formerly Mormon.

—My denomination has gone from zero churches in eastern Idaho to ten in five years.

Christian radio and television are reaching into Mormon homes and account for some of the change in Mormondom. But mainly, people are just fed up with oppression. One Mormon put it to me in these graphic terms: "I'm tired of being treated like a mushroom; they keep me in the dark and feed me manure."

Recent developments have cost the Mormon Church thousands of members. I predict tens of thousands of others will leave Mormonism in the next few years. Three of the most important factors causing defections are:

First, the fall of the Book of Mormon to the archaeologists and anthropologists (see Chapter Ten).

Second, the continual uncovering of the shady early Church history. Particularly the mounting evidence for the occult activities of Joseph Smith. That Joseph Smith was heavily into witchcraft is, in my estimation, the worst problem for the Church he founded.

Third, the Mormon Church's cover-up of the above. Thousands of Mormons were demoralized to discover that acting President of the Church Gordon B. Hinckley was involved in the purchase of controversial historical papers from rare-documents dealer Mark Hofmann. Many were convinced the reason Hinckley bought them was to suppress them. Ironically, though Hofmann is a member of the Church, most of the documents he sold to Hinckley were forgeries. (Hofmann, at the time of this writing, is on trial for murder and forgery in Utah.)

Three Escape Routes

In the face of all this unpleasantness, there are three primary reactions:

First, the fundamentalist reaction. Some Mormons harden their faith in the face of mounting damning evidence. They see the problems, but refuse to face them. These fundamentalists choose not to think about the implications of what they see. A Mormon bishop friend said to me, "Well, if I find out Mormonism is wrong when I die, at least I'll have the satisfaction of knowing I lived a good life."

Second, there is the flight to liberalism. Those who choose this path commit intellectual suicide.

These are Mormon intellectuals who redefine their theology in the face of historical discovery and attempt to forge a Brave New Mormonism. Typical of this group is former Church historian Leonard J. Arrington who has said it is no longer important to him if Joseph Smith had *any* of the visions he said he had. Joseph's stories, according to Arrington, "convey truth," *whether or not they are actually true.* Quoting an Italian proverb Arrington says, "Whether it is *literally* true or not, it's still true."

Third, there are Mormons who ask, "Is anything salvageable in Mormonism?" Some then jettison everything except Jesus Christ, which leads them to orthodox Christianity.

Those who opt for Christianity are those who deal honestly with unpleasant facts. For example, Mormons are now asked to deal with historical evidence confirming Joseph Smith's involvement in witchcraft. The fundamentalists say it isn't so; the Liberals say it doesn't matter; but the honest see that they must reexamine the roots of their faith.

When Latter-day Saints finally capitulate to the evidence, it can be a very traumatic experience. They are brokenhearted. Some are angry. Most are disoriented. I have received letters from hundreds who tell me of the anguish they experience leaving the Church. All leave loved ones behind.

Some feel used, like the man who described giving his whole life to Mormonism—thousands of dollars and years of service. And, ultimately, he gave his children. It is understandable that it may take months or years to overcome feelings of bitterness.

Then there is the spiritual intimidation. Many exiting Mormons experience months of inexplicable fear. In fact nearly all the former Mormons I know—especially former temple Mormons (people who have passed through secret occult initiation rites) say that they have had bouts with bone-chilling fear. Many have demonic visitations, some in the form of dead relatives who beg them to return to the Church. (If anyone reading this is suffering from demonic oppression, pray right now that the shed blood of Jesus will protect you. Then get to a good Bible-believing church and get men and women of God to pray for you.)

Others report impaired mental faculties. Over and over again I hear, "Pastor, I just can't think straight." One man said his own handwriting became so garbled he could barely read it. One lady thought she was being poisoned because she developed terrible physical symptoms. (See Appendix D: "Psychological Snapping in the Cults.")

Harassment is also financial. People lose their jobs. Friends of mine, former Mormons who were responsible for much of the revival in Vernal, Utah, lost a prosperous business when they left the Church because Mormons would no longer patronize their store.

There is only one power on earth that can salve the loss and rejection a Latter-day Saint experiences when he leaves the faith: the power of Jesus. The exiting Mormon must find Jesus Christ as personal Lord and Savior. He must be born again. When he experiences the new birth, he is empowered to endure. Recently a thirty-five-year-old man, the father of five, read my book, *Beyond Mormonism,* and simultaneously befriended a born-again Christian. After months of study, he found Christ. One day Don told me that his wife, frustrated by his conversion, was seeking divorce with the approval of his Stake President who explained that by leaving the Church he had forced his wife to "look for someone else who can take her to the celestial kingdom."

At this time, it appears Don and his wife will divorce. In spite of faithful prayer by Don and many supportive Christian friends, finally the decision rests with his wife.

There is no way to explain the grace God gives those who choose to be obedient to Jesus. Those who have not had to make the choice between family and God cannot comprehend the flow of grace in that moment. Through the tears there is a very real sense of the presence of God and we come to know by experience the Scripture that says, "God is a very real help in time of trouble."

Don told me, "Brother, this is the pits. But, I know I am cradled in the arms of Jesus. I know I can take whatever the future holds for me." There is no turning back for Don. He has decided to follow Jesus.

If you are involved in helping Mormons leave the Church, you will need to be very sympathetic, understanding, and patient as the Latter-day Saint finds his or her way through the maze into the open air.

After years of study, conversations with Mormons, and my own personal experience, I believe Mormons must spiritually break with Mormonism before they are able to come to Christ.

I know people who disagree with me on this point. They think, they hope that God will move through the Mormon Church and convert people to Christ and allow them to remain Mormons. I don't think that will happen; I don't think it *can* happen.

The biblical example is that one must leave Egypt before he can come into the Promised Land. "I brought you out to bring you in," the Lord declares. Egypt could not be converted. Neither can Mormonism. The foundations are as the foundations of Babylon. Mormons must leave Mormonism before it falls into the abyss.

Church history teaches us that false religion, like all mediocre ideas, is doomed to failure, because it cannot sustain enthusiasm. Throughout the history of the Church of Jesus Christ, spurious groups, once they had broken with Christian orthodoxy, followed a path of decline to oblivion:

—The Donatists are no more.

—The Gnostics survive only on the arcane fringes of the occult.

—The spiritualists—as Abraham Lincoln said of slavery—glowed for a time; but their wicks went out and they "stank in the dark" for a season before slipping into oblivion.

—Christian Science, once the darling of the intelligentsia, is now a religion of old ladies and I believe it will be dead in a generation; Swedenborgianism is a joke; Scientology is foundationless; and the foundations of the Zion Curtain are cracking.

Mormonism is at the beginning of decline. It is, in spite of its monolithic facade, crumbling, falling from the inside out. It must, according to the Bible, like all the children of Babylon, fall, "and great will be the fall thereof."

Our word to those who inhabit her borders must be: "Come out of her! Flee the wrath to come!"

As Mormons come out into the sunshine of God's love and into the kingdom of light, it is our great privilege to know, love, and teach exiting Mormons.

I challenge you to be one who joins me in loving Mormons enough to tell them they have a terminal doctrinal disease. I challenge you to join me in helping them find safe havens and fellowship and pastors who will feed them.

Will you help me free my people, God's beloved lost Latter-day Saints?

Chapter Sixteen

How to Resign from the Mormon Church

> "I am afraid of the pressure that I know the ward can put on me.... I don't want to be excommunicated. I just want to drop out quietly if I can."
>
> **Roger**

It is important for exiting Mormons to break connection with the Church. It is necessary for several reasons.

First, unless a person actually *resigns,* the Mormon Church will carry his name on its membership roll forever. Even if they haven't been to church for thirty years. Exiting Mormons who remove their names bring the Church growth numbers closer to the truth. This is important because many people investigating Mormonism are unduly impressed by the "numbers."

Second, by resigning membership in the Church, the exiting Mormon is delivering an important message to others. The action says, "I am *not* a Mormon, and I think something is *wrong* with Mormonism." I wonder how many bishops are amazed at the letters requesting excommunication that cross their desks.

Third, I think an important spiritual connection is broken when one breaks with the Mormon Church. A Mormon convert voluntarily places himself under Mormon authority and, hence, the spirit of Mormonism. Resigning breaks the spiritual connection. I know many people who have had a very real emotional release after verbally renouncing, then formally resigning from the Mormon Church.

Resigning can be accomplished by mail. *You do not have to attend what is known as "excommunication court."* But, the letter needs to be firm, and it needs to be mailed to three people:

1. The bishop of the Mormon Ward the Latter-day Saint *currently resides* in. If the bishop says he doesn't have those records, insist that he get them.

2. The Stake President of the Stake of residence.

3. Finally, the President of the Mormon Church. *Be sure that each copy of the letter lists all the others receiving copies.* The President of the Church can be reached in care of The Church Office Building, Salt Lake City, Utah.

The resignation letter must be strong. But it should be your own words. Here is a sample letter:

Dear Bishop (Stake President, President):

This letter is to inform you that I wish to resign from the Church, and request that my name be stricken from the records of the Church of Jesus Christ of Latter-day Saints.

I have made this decision with full understanding. I am operating within the constitutional religious freedom guaranteed a citizen of the United States.

I insist that the Church record show that the *only* reason for terminating membership is my request of resignation. And I request a letter to that effect be sent to me. I will not hesitate to take immediate legal action against you personally, and the Church corporately, if anything is done to libel my name or cause me any loss of reputation. I further insist that you honor my request *in a timely manner.*

Copies of this letter have been sent to the bishop of the ward within whose boundaries I reside, the President of the Stake, and the President of the Church of Jesus Christ of Latter-day Saints.

I take this action because I'm fully persuaded that the Mormon Church is in great error, teaches false doctrine, and greatly displeases God.

I believe that Joseph Smith was a false prophet. He failed every major test as to the validity of his office according to Deuteronomy 18:20–22 and Galatians 1:8. Further, I do not have confidence in any of the successive prophets of the Church since Smith's time.

I do not think the gospel has been "restored" because I don't think it was "lost from the earth." Jesus said the gates of hell would never prevail against His Church, and I don't think they ever did.

I am convinced the Book of Mormon is not of divine origin, but a text Smith copied from the King James Bible and secular writings as a fraud to get financial gain and power over the lives of others.

I find the "Law of Eternal Progression" in direct conflict with Isaiah chapters 43–46, Deuteronomy 6:4, and Job chapters 38–42.

I have many other doctrinal differences with the Church. I do not believe in baptism for the dead, the authority of the Mormon priesthood, or the three levels of heaven.

Since I have become born again through faith in Christ and that alone, I have become aware that all Mormon doctrine is tainted with error.

I have come to this decision after prayer, and it is absolutely final. Any attempt to contact me to change my thinking, by Home Teachers, Visiting Teachers, Missionaries, or other representatives of the LDS Church, I would consider an invasion of my privacy.

Since I have done nothing wrong, I will participate in no Church court or trial.

I have obtained great peace of mind since coming to a knowledge of my Lord and Savior, Jesus Christ. I have assurance that my salvation is not dependent upon my own futile attempts at righteousness, but on Christ. *He* is my salvation.

I would personally encourage you to examine again the first eight chapters of the book of Romans, the book of Galatians, and the second chapter of the book of Ephesians.

I pray for your salvation.

Sincerely,
(Signature)

Appendices

Appendix A

The Book of Mormon and the Nature of God

Mormonism is polytheistic but, ironically, the Book of Mormon is *not*. The following verses are typical of what the Book of Mormon says about the nature of God. Nothing here sounds like the "plurality of gods" which currently is taught by the Mormon Church.

> And as I spake concerning the convincing of the Jews, that Jesus is the very Christ, it must needs be that the gentiles be convinced also that Jesus is the Christ, the Eternal God (II Nephi 26:12).

> And now, behold, this is the doctrine of Christ and the only and true doctrine of the Father, and of the Son, and of the Holy Ghost, which is one God, without end, Amen (II Nephi 31:21).

> And because he said unto them that Christ was the God, the Father of all things, and said that he should take upon him the image of man ... and that God should come down among the children of men, and take upon him flesh and blood, and go forth upon the face of the earth—(Mosiah 7:27).

> And now Abinadi said unto them: I would that ye should understand that God himself shall come down among the children of men, and shall redeem his people.

And because he dwelleth in the flesh he shall be called the Son of God, and having subjected the flesh to the will of the Father, being the Father and the Son—

The Father because he was conceived by the power of God; and the Son; because of the flesh; thus becoming the Father and Son—

And they are one God, yea, the very Eternal Father of heaven and of earth (Mosiah 15:1-4).

Teach them that redemption cometh through Christ the Lord, who is the very Eternal Father (Mosiah 16:15).

Now Zeezrom saith again unto him: Is the Son of God the very Eternal Father?

And Amulek said unto him: Yea, he is the very Eternal Father of heaven and of earth, and all things which in them are; he is the beginning and the end, the first and the last (Alma 11:38-39).

Behold, I am Jesus Christ. I am the Father and the Son (Ether 3:14).

Jesus is the Christ, the Eternal God (Title page, Book of Mormon).

And honor be to the Father, and to the Son, and to the Holy Ghost, which is one God. Amen (The Testimony of Three Witnesses, Book of Mormon).

From *Doctrine and Covenants:*

Which Father, Son and Holy Ghost are one God, infinite and eternal, without end. Amen (Sec. 20, vs. 28).

Appendix B

Brigham H. Roberts: Mormon Giant Who Lost Confidence in the Book of Mormon

Brigham H. Roberts was one of the Mormon Church's greatest theologians and historians. He was author of the six-volume *Comprehensive History of the Church*, still one of the most respected works of Mormon history. He was in his time recognized as *the* expert Mormon apologist and in 1909 he published his chief defense of the Book of Mormon, entitled *New Witnesses for God*. He was a General Authority and a member of the then powerful First Council of the Seventy.

In 1921 an event occurred that forever changed Roberts' life. Roberts was asked to answer a man investigating Mormonism who asked five questions (given below) about the Book of Mormon. Roberts began an investigation that would trouble him until his death in 1933. The study deeply challenged his faith in the Book of Mormon.

The depth of Roberts' personal struggle over the matter is recorded in three documents he produced in the years before he died. None of these works was published during Roberts' lifetime, but they are now available. (A comprehensive study of these documents is published as *Studies of* the *Book of Mormon,* University of Illinois Press, Urbana, Illinois.)

As his struggle intensified, Roberts wrote an open letter to President Heber J. Grant, to Grant's counselors, to The Twelve Apostles and to the First Council of Seventy, requesting an emergency meeting with all of them to discuss the matter.

President Grant immediately assembled the brethren for two days of intense meetings at which Roberts delivered a 141-page report entitled "Book of Mormon Difficulties, A Study." Roberts asked for the collective wisdom of the brethren and the inspiration of the Lord in order to answer the questions.

Roberts had hoped to find answers at the meeting, but he came away after the two days disappointed and discouraged. As his investigation continued, he became more and more disillusioned with the Book of Mormon. Two months before his death he told a friend, Wesley P. Lloyd, former dean of the graduate school of BYU, that the defense the brethren made for the Book of Mormon might "satisfy people who didn't think, but [it was] a very inadequate answer for a thinking man." Roberts told Lloyd he did not criticize the brethren for not being able to answer the questions, but said, *"In a Church which claimed continuous revelation, a crisis had arisen where revelation was necessary."* But it was not forthcoming. Here are the five questions the prophets could not answer:

First, linguistics. The investigator asked why, if the American Indians were all descendants of Lehi, there was such a diversity in the languages of the American Indians and why was there no indication of Hebrew in any of the Indian languages.

Second, the Book of Mormon says that Lehi found horses when he arrived in America. The horse described in the Book of Mormon did not exist here. It was imported with the Spaniards in the sixteenth century.

Third, Nephi is stated to have had a "bow of steel." Jews did not know steel at that time. And there was no iron smelted on this continent until after the Spaniard colonization.

Fourth, the Book of Mormon mentions "swords and cimeters." Scimitars are unknown until the rise of the Moslem faith, after 500 A.D.

Fifth, the Book of Mormon says the Nephites possessed silk. Silk did not exist in America in pre-Columbian times.

At first, Roberts was most concerned about the linguistic problem. But as he studied, he discovered *new* problems. He told Lloyd he saw *literary* problems in the Book of Mormon as well as *geographic* problems. Where were the Mayan cliffs and high mountain peaks from the Book of Mormon? The geography of the Book of Mormon looked suspiciously like the New England of Joseph Smith.

Roberts eventually concluded: That Joseph Smith wrote the Book of Mormon himself, that he did *not* translate it from gold plates, and that he produced the Book of Mormon by drawing upon materials like Ethan Smith's *View of the Hebrews,* published near Joseph's home a few years before the "translation " of the Book of Mormon. Roberts became convinced that *View of the Hebrews* was "the ground plan" for the Book of Mormon.

Incredibly, Brigham Roberts, who started his career defending the Book of Mormon and became its staunchest apologist, had to admit that Joseph Smith was a plagiarist. One can sympathize with the elderly Roberts who realized he had spent a lifetime defending something he came to see as fraud. It was heartbreaking. Roberts also investigated "the imaginative mind of Joseph Smith." He concluded that Joseph could have made up most of the Book of Mormon out of his own mind. He quoted Joseph's mother as she recalled how Joseph would give "amusing recitals" in which he would describe "the ancient inhabitants of this continent, their dress, mode of traveling, and the animals upon which they rode; their cities, their buildings, with every particular; their mode of warfare; and also their religious worship." All this, Roberts acknowledged, "took place *before* the young prophet had received the plates of the Book of Mormon."

The Book of Mormon, he argued, must be of human origin. And if it is, so must be the rest of the work of Joseph Smith. "His revelations become merely human productions. . . ."

Roberts suggested that Smith became caught up in spiritual "excesses" out of which he imagined prophecies and manifestations. Roberts concluded that Smith's visions were "psychological" and that the gold plates "were not objective"—that is, they didn't exist.

Appendix C

Solomon Spalding's Manuscript and the Book of Mormon

One of the persistent theories for the origin of the Book of Mormon is "The Spalding Theory": that the Book of Mormon is derived from a document written by a Congregational preacher named Solomon Spalding. Spalding wrote what he termed a "romantic novel" about the ancient inhabitants of this continent. In Spalding's novel these inhabitants were descended from a band of Hebrews who migrated from Jerusalem in 600 B.C. Spalding finished his manuscript about 1812, nearly twenty years before Joseph Smith published the Book of Mormon.

Contemporaries of Spalding, who heard him read his manuscript before he tried to get it published, claimed it was unquestionably the source document for the Book of Mormon. They remember hearing Spalding read the names, places, and events later published in the Book of Mormon—names like Nephi, Lehi, Laban, and Moroni.

Spalding's story recounted the drama of the Jews sailing to the Western Hemisphere in barges, and then dividing into two antagonistic groups, one righteous and the other idolatrous. These two factions fought and warred until, in the end, the righteous Nephites were destroyed by the Lamanites. All the righteous were slain except one who kept and concealed the records of his group.

Immediately upon publication of the Book of Mormon in 1830, Spalding's relatives and friends came forward charging Joseph Smith with plagiarism and fraud.

Spalding's widow said her husband had written the novel as entertainment and to occupy his time while he lingered in ill health. Spalding, an ordained minister and a graduate of Dartmouth College, had suffered financial reverses. His problems, coupled with a growing interest in the manuscript among friends, prompted him to attempt to have the manuscript published. He took the book to a printer in Pittsburgh but unfortunately before publication, on October 20, 1816, Spalding died.

Spalding's widow, his brother, and numerous acquaintances claimed that the Book of Mormon, which appeared in 1830, was nothing more than a thinly disguised version of *Manuscript Found.* When a Mormon missionary came to New Salem, Ohio, in 1834 and began holding meetings, Solomon's brother John attended. As the missionary began reading portions of the Book of Mormon, John immediately identified it as his brother's novel.

Numerous witnesses swore that the Book of Mormon was a plagiarism. E. D. Howe published, *just four years after the publication of the Book of Mormon,* a short history of the development of Mormonism, including statements from friends, relatives, and acquaintances of Solomon Spalding. All of the witnesses said the Book of Mormon was a plagiarism of *Manuscript Found.*

The following statement was made by Spalding's brother John, who, according to Spalding's widow, Matilda, was an "extremely pious man":

> He [Solomon] then told me he was writing a book. . . . It was an historical romance of the first settlers of America, endeavoring to show that the American Indians are the de-

scendants of the Jews, or the lost tribes. It gave a detailed account of their journey from Jerusalem, by land and sea, till they arrived in America, under the command of Nephi and Lehi. They afterwards had quarrels and contentions and separated into two distinct nations, one of which he denominated Nephites, and the other Lamanites. Cruel and bloody wars ensued, in which great multitudes were slain. They buried their dead in large heaps, which caused the mounds so common in this country. Their arts, sciences and civilization were brought into view in order to account for all the curious antiquities found in various parts of North and South America. I have recently read the Book of Mormon and to my great surprise I find nearly the same historical matter, names, &c., as they were in my brother's writings. I well remember that he wrote in the old style, and commenced about every sentence with 'And it came to pass,' or 'Now it came to pass,' the same as the Book of Mormon, and according to the best of my recollection and belief, it is the same as my brother Solomon wrote, with the exception of the religious part. By what means it has fallen into the hands of Joseph Smith, Jr., I am unable to determine.[1]

Here is the statement of Spalding's wife, Matilda:

Mr. Spalding . . . in order to beguile the hours of retirement and furnish employment for his lively imagination . . . conceived the idea of giving an historical account of a long lost race. . . . His sole object in writing this historical romance was to amuse himself and his neighbors.[2]

The statement of Spalding's sister-in-law Martha:

[Spalding] had for many years contended that the aborigines of America were the descendants of some of the lost tribes of Israel and this idea he carried out in the book in

1.   Howe, pp. 279–280.
2.   *The Boston Recorder*, May 18, 1839.

question. . . . The names of Nephi and Lehi are yet fresh in my memory, as being the principal heroes of his tale.[3]

The statement of Spalding's busines partner, Henry Lake, who partnered with Spalding in an iron forge in Conneaut County, Ohio, during the time of the writing of the manuscript:

Some months ago, I borrowed the Golden Bible, put it into my pocket, carried it home, and thought no more of it. About a week after, my wife found the book in my coat pocket, as it hung up, and she commenced reading it aloud as I lay upon the bed. She had not read twenty minutes, till I was astonished to find the same passages in it that Spalding had read to me more than twenty years before, from his 'Manuscript Found.' Since then, I have more fully examined the said Golden Bible, and have no hesitation in saying that the historical part of it is principally, if not wholly, taken from the 'Manuscript Found.' I well recollect telling Mr. Spalding that the so frequent use of the words 'And it came to pass,' and 'Now it came to pass,' rendered it ridiculous.[4]

The statement of John N. Miller, one of Spalding's former employees, who thought the whole book was "humorous":

I have recently examined the Book of Mormon, and find in it the writings of Solomon Spalding, from beginning to end, but mixed up with Scripture and other religious matter, which I did not meet with in the 'Manuscript Found.' Many of the passages in the Mormon book are verbatim from Spalding, and others in part. The names of Nephi, Lehi, Moroni, and in fact all the principal names are brought fresh to my recollection by the Golden Bible. When Spalding divested his history of its fabulous names, by a verbal explanation, he landed his people near the Straits of

3. Howe, p. 280.
4. Howe, pp. 281–282.

Darien, which I am very confident he called Zarahemla; they were marched about that country for a length of time, in which wars and great bloodshed ensued; he brought them across North America in a northeast direction.[5]

The statement of one of Spalding's creditors, Artemas Cunningham:

His only hope of ever paying his debts appeared to be upon the sale of a book he had been writing.... [he said] that it was a fabulous or romantic history.... It purported to have been a record found buried in the earth.... He had adopted the ancient or scripture style of writing.... I well remember the name of Nephi, which appeared to be the principal hero of the story. The frequent repetition of the phrase, 'I Nephi,' I recollect as distinctly as though it was but yesterday.... The Mormon Bible I have partially examined, and am fully of the opinion that Solomon Spalding had written its outlines before he left Conneaut.[6]

The statement of Aaron Wright, Justice of the Peace in Conneaut, a man of droll humor, who when he heard the Book of Mormon read in a public meeting in Conneaut in 1832 remarked, "Old Come-to-Pass has come to life again!":

The historical part of the Book of Mormon I know to be the same as I read and heard read from the writings of Spalding, more than twenty years ago; the names, more especially, are the same without any alteration.... Spalding had many other manuscripts, which I expect to see when Smith translates his other plate.... If it is not Spalding's writing, it is the same as he wrote; and if Smith was inspired, I think it was by the same spirit that Spalding was, which confessed to be the love of money.[7]

5. Howe, p. 283.
6. Howe, pp. 286-287.
7. Howe, p. 284.

The statement of Dr. Nahum Howard, town doctor of Conneaut:

> I have lately read the Book of Mormon, and believe it to be the same as Spalding wrote, except for the religious part.[8]

The Lost Manuscript

Sidney Rigdon was born in Library, Pennsylvania, in 1793. In 1812, when he was nineteen, he moved to Pittsburgh to find work. There he befriended a J. H. Lambdin who worked as a printer at R. and J. Patterson's Print Shop.

Coincidentally, Spalding moved to Pittsburgh and contacted this same Patterson to see if he would publish *Manuscript Found*. Patterson was interested, but he delayed the undertaking. Before Spalding died, in 1816, Patterson told him the manuscript had been lost.

But Spalding thought the manuscript had been stolen. He told Dr. Cephas Dodd, the physician who attended him during his final illness, that Sidney Rigdon had stolen it. He said the same thing to the Rev. Joseph Miller who made Spalding's coffin and superintended his burial. Both men have left signed statements to that effect. Fourteen years later, the manuscript surfaced as the Book of Mormon.

Meanwhile, Rigdon's religious career was taking off. In 1817 he joined the First Baptist Church near his hometown of Library. A year or so later he was called to preach and soon married. In 1822 he became minister at First Baptist Church in Pittsburgh, but he was excommunicated in 1823 for teaching "irregular doctrine."

While pastoring in Pittsburgh, he was friendly with a Dr. J. Winter who asserted that Rigdon had showed him the Spalding manuscript.

Rigdon later became a Campbellite preacher (Disciples of Christ). Before the Book of Mormon was published, Rigdon

8. Howe, p. 286.

told his brother-in-law, Adamson Bently (also a Campbellite preacher), about gold plates found in New York, which would be the source for a new book. Bently believed that Rigdon and Joseph Smith cooked up Mormonism between them to "deceive the people and obtain their property."

Even Alexander Campbell, the founder of the Disciples of Christ, reports hearing Rigdon speak of the gold plates before the Book of Mormon was published.

Rigdon supposedly was converted to Mormonism in Ohio in 1830 when traveling Mormon missionaries baptized him in Kirtland. He immediately went to Joseph Smith in Fayette, New York, where they supposedly met for the first time. He returned to head up the Mormon Church in Kirtland. Soon the entire Mormon Church moved to Kirtland. Rigdon became a member of the First Presidency and continued in that position until he left the Mormon Church after Smith's death in 1844.

Once again, however, things were not what they seemed, for several witnesses testify that Rigdon had visited the Smith farm many times *before* the Book of Mormon was published. Abel D. Chase leaves this testimony:

> During some of my visits at the Smiths, I saw a stranger there who they said was Mr. Rigdon. He was at Smith's several times, and it was in the year of 1827 [the Book of Mormon was published in 1830] when I first saw him there, as near as I can recollect. Some time after that tales were circulated that young Joe had found or dug from the earth a Book of Plates which the Smiths called the Golden Bible. I don't think Smith had any such plates. He was mysterious in his actions. The Peepstone, in which he was accustomed to look, he got off my elder brother Willard while at work for us digging a well. It was a singular looking stone and young Joe pretended he could discover hidden things in it.[9]

9. *Mormon Portraits,* W. Wyl, pp. 230–231, as cited by Cowdery, Davis, & Scales, p. 126.

The Moving Finger Writes!

Historians have long hoped to find the original Spalding manuscript, in order to prove once and for all that it was the source for the Book of Mormon. Thus far, the manuscript appears to have been lost or destroyed.

In February 1976 an amazing thing happened. A Mormon researcher, Howard Davis, who had been working for years trying to locate *Manuscript Found!*, was home from work, ill. He was absently flipping through a Mormon research book when suddenly he spotted a distinctive handwriting, which he recognized from earlier research. It was Solomon Spalding's writing! He was sure of it. "What is Spalding's handwriting doing here?" he asked himself. *Davis was looking at a photocopy of a section of the original transcription of the Book of Mormon.* The original document was housed in Salt Lake City in the vault of the history office of the Mormon Church.

The Book of Mormon had been dictated by Joseph Smith to various scribes. The scribes were separated from him by a curtain so they "could not see the gold plates." The original manuscript had been closely guarded by Smith until 1841, three years before his death, when he deposited it in the cornerstone of his Nauvoo, Illinois, mansion, Nauvoo House.

In 1882 workmen dismantled the house and found the manuscript in a chest in the cornerstone. The Mormon Church possesses 144 pages of the manuscript. It was a photocopy of some of these pages that Davis saw and immediately recognized as Spalding's handwriting.

Could it be that Joseph Smith had simply inserted a portion of the actual Spalding manuscript into the original Book of Mormon manuscript? It seems a little too daring, even for Smith, but we need to bear in mind that when the Book of Mormon was published in 1830, Spalding had been dead for

16 years. Rigdon and Smith, after such a long period of time, probably felt that no one would ever remember the obscure preacher or his romantic novel.

The Mormon Church had attempted, in 1970, to identify the various sections they possessed of the Book of Mormon manuscript. Several handwritings were identified in the manuscript. The portion Davis recognized was from twelve manuscript pages labeled by the Church as "the unidentified scribe section."

The Church was outraged that Davis would suggest that "the unidentified scribe section" was the handwriting of none other than Solomon Spalding.

Davis called in a respected handwriting expert, William Kayne, and had him compare Spalding's handwriting with "the unidentified scribe section." Kayne (although his findings were contested) said that Spalding was the "unidentified scribe."

The Mormon Church could clear up the issue easily. All they have to do is make the manuscript available for independent examination. A consensus could be reached immediately. But they refuse to let anyone examine the documents. They are buried in a vault in the Church Office Building.

In view of all the existing testimony and evidence, it seems that the Spalding Theory is still alive and offers one explanation for at least part of the manuscript that Joseph Smith published as the Book of Mormon. What Spalding began as an innocent "romantic novel" may have become the central source for one of the most notorious cults in the history of Christianity.

I suggest interested persons read *Who Really Wrote the Book of Mormon?*, by Davis, Cowdrey, and Scales (Vision House, Santa Ana, California). One of these men is Wayne Cowdrey, a descendant of one of the Three Witnesses to the

Book of Mormon. Cowdrey, along with Dr. Howard Davis
and Donald Scales, documented with relentless accuracy the
saga of the Spalding Theory or what they prefer to term the
Rigdon/Spalding Thesis.

Appendix D

Psychological "Snapping" in the Cults

Certain interesting phenomena occur in the "snapped" person. For one thing, investigators find that a person's intellectual maturity seems to freeze at the point he entered the cult. Former cult members leave the cult at about the same psychological age they entered.[1]

I had always been an excited learner, feeling I was growing in maturity, experience, and emotional stature. During my ten years as a Mormon, however, I had the nagging feeling I was going nowhere. Now, after nearly ten years of post-Mormon experience, I am once again experiencing the exciting feeling of personal growth.

People leaving cults also tend to experience a period of "withdrawal" in which they fight confusion. For several years after I left Mormonism, I experienced a frustrating sensation that there were places in my mind I could not go. In trying to talk to people about it, I described what seemed to be a steel band wrapped tightly around my mind.

Only after considerable ministry and prayer did I experience complete deliverance from the hold of the Mormon cult. As a final act of rejecting Mormonism, I took all Mormon literature out of my home and burned several

1. Flo Conway and Jim Siegelman, *Science Digest,* "Information Disease: Have Cults Created a New Mental Illness?" January 1982, pp. 86–92.

dozen books in the desert. Only then did I feel completely free.

Studies indicate that the average rehabilitation time for former cult members is sixteen months. Long-term effects include recurring nightmares and becoming "unable to think."

Resource Groups

Dr. Walter Martin
The Christian Research Institute
P.O. Box 500
San Juan Capistrano, CA 92675

Ed Decker
Saints Alive
P.O. Box 1076
Issaquah, WA 98027

Jerald and Sandra Tanner
Utah Lighthouse Ministry
P.O. Box 1884
Salt Lake City, UT 84110

Spiritual Counterfeits Project
P.O. Box 4309
Berkeley, CA 94704

James R. Spencer

To contact James R. Spencer or to receive the newsletter, *Through the Maze:*

James R. Spencer
Through the Maze
P.O. Box 3804
Idaho Falls, ID 83403